Embattled Wall

AMERICANS UNITED: *An Idea and a Man*
by C. Stanley Lowell

Author C. Stanley Lowell, Associate Director of Americans United, and
Glenn L. Archer, Executive Director, at the organization's headquarters,
1633 Massachusetts Avenue, N. W., Washington, D.C.

AMERICANS UNITED • WASHINGTON, D. C.

Library of Congress Catalog Card Number 66-24865

CONTENTS

This book is for—

HAROLD C. FITZ
Rear Admiral, United States Navy *(Retired)*

Whose steady hand has guided us and whose unfaltering trust has made us strong.

PREFACE

The 20th anniversary of a movement would seem to be a good time to appraise its balance sheet. Here is half a generation, an appropriate moment to survey assets and liabilities, to note successes and to dissect failures. The story of 20 years is by no means the full story, but it is enough of it to be significant. Here are sufficient points to plot a curve.

The story of AMERICANS UNITED, often referred to as POAU, is obviously an inside job. The organization is approaching its 20th birthday. I have been associated with it nearly that long. While not among the founders, I served on the original National Advisory Council and was, I believe, the first non-founder to be named to the Board of Trustees. After nearly a decade in this association, I joined the staff as associate director and editor in 1956.

This is a work of love. I am devoted to my job. I believe that the effort of Americans United is highly important to the health of the nation. My work is so fascinating that I would gladly pay Americans United for the privilege of performing it if I could afford it. All of this will naturally be reflected in these pages. But there is a valid place, I believe, for this kind of history. It can tell as no other kind could what really went on inside. It can reflect the thinking of the men who were in actual charge of the movement during its formative years. It can present close up their reaction to church-state events spanning nearly two decades.

I am indebted to Miss Adele Porter of our editorial staff for patient assistance in research and in the preparation of the index and to my secretary, Mrs. Elaine Bowers, for assistance in the same work and for her meticulous typing of the manuscript. My heaviest obligation is, no doubt, to our Director Glenn L. Archer, whose work so largely made the story recorded here.

Glenn L. Archer, Executive Director, Protestants and Other Americans
United for the Separation of Church and State.

chapter I THE EVENT

The nineteen-sixties have been characterized by a burgeoning controversy over public aid to parochial schools. This issue has become the focal point of the struggle over separation of church and state in the United States. The controversy over it is steadily growing in scope and intensity.

This church-state issue has had some strange turns and twists. President Kennedy, a Roman Catholic, won election on a promise to refuse Federal assistance to parochial schools. President Johnson, a Protestant, sponsored legislation which marked a breakthrough in Federal aid to parochial schools.

The attack on church-state separation via public subsidy to parochial schools has proceeded apace in the states. New York State today is pondering constitutional changes which would make possible full public subsidy to parochial schools. Many states are presently convulsed with controversies over the same issue.

All of this was just beginning when a fledgling organization designed to defend separation of church and state came into being in 1947. Indeed, that year might well have marked the commencement of the latest phase of this age-old controversy involving relations between the state and the church.

The year 1947 was critical for church-state relations in the United States. It marked the one hundredth anniversary of the effort of Archbishop John Hughes of New York to secure tax funds for the support of Roman Catholic denominational schools in that state. Archbishop Hughes had also organized a church political party to further his ambition for public subsidy. The Catholic prelate was repudiated at the polls; his party disintegrated and New York State wrote into its constitution some of the strictest prohibitions on the use of public funds for church schools that are to be found in any such document. The archbishop told his co-religionists in the throes of their defeat that they must build up their own school system.[1]

By 1947, Roman Catholic leaders felt that the time had come to demand recognition and support of the state for a denominational school system that then numbered some 4 million students at the elementary and secondary levels. In 1947, Father William E. McManus, who then headed the educational division of the National Catholic Welfare Conference, went before a subcommittee of the House Committee on Education and Labor to state the Catholic position on Federal aid to parochial schools. He expressed it thus:

The financing of schools through public taxation is a responsibility of government, especially of local and state governments. This responsibility entails an obligation to observe the norms of distributive justice in distributing tax funds among the schools within the community. Since government itself has nothing to teach, and because government receives a full return from its educational investment when a school produces well-trained citizens, therefore, every school to which parents may send their children in compliance with the compulsory education laws of the State is entitled to a fair share of tax funds. Local, and State governments which refuse to support schools not under the control of the local school board are guilty of an injustice against other qualified schools within the community.[2]

This has always been the official Catholic position on school aid. It remains so. It is true that the Catholic leadership has tactically pressed and retreated in its demands as expediency indicated the proper course. But of the end result sought there could be no doubt. What was sought was complete public subsidy for the Catholic school system.

Any doubt on this point was erased in the following year when the Roman Catholic bishops of the United States themselves issued an official pronouncement on the subject. This statement, released by the National Catholic Welfare Conference on Nov. 21, 1948, made a frontal attack on the Supreme Court doctrine enunciated in the *McCollum* case which barred religious schools from receiving public subsidies.[3] The bishops attacked such a doctrine as an "establishment of secularism" and urged their people to work "peacefully, patiently and perseveringly" to supplant it with another concept under which religious schools could receive public subsidies.

The Catholic position on school aid has not changed since that pronouncement. There have, to be sure, been some downs and ups and strategically enjoined retreats and advances. These shifts were made necessary by the ebb and flow of public opinion. They are mirrored in the public position on school aid assumed from time to time by Cardinal Francis Spellman, Catholic Archbishop of New York, who has long been his church's best known spokesman in the United States. In 1949 Cardinal Spellman made a public attack on Mrs. Eleanor Roosevelt because she had opposed government subsidy to religious schools. In the resulting furor public opinion turned against the cardinal and it became advisable for him to retreat from the stiff position he had taken. He did so by asserting that all he had ever wanted for Catholic schools was "welfare" benefits, not full public subsidy.

The Catholic press never let up in its demands, however. It incessantly campaigned not for mere auxiliary benefits or welfare aid for Catholic students but for full public subsidy of Catholic schools. Indeed, Cardinal Spellman himself, after a reasonable period, resumed his original demands and also his role as the principal protagonist of government aid for Catholic schools. In 1960 we find him actually engaging in an angry controversy with President John F. Kennedy, first Catholic ever to be elected to that high office, over this very issue. The official Catholic position on school aid as enunciated by Father McManus in 1947 has been often reiterated and consistently supported by the Catholic leadership ever since. Americans long lulled into security by the apparent acceptance of the separation of church and state by all groups, have gradually awakened to the painful realization that a new force was at work among them seeking quite another goal. The separation arrangement was jeopardized by militant advocacy of a tax to support religious schools. For the first time in 150 years the tax for religion loomed as a serious possibility.

Nineteen-forty-seven brought other disturbing developments. This was the year of the Supreme Court decision in the famous *Everson* bus case. This case concerned a rebate on bus tickets paid by a New Jersey community to parents of parochial school children for their transportation to these institutions. In a five to four decision, the Court held that this arrangement did not violate the First Amendment. What the Court really attempted to do in the *Everson* case was to yield a little to Catholic demands, then set positive limits beyond which these demands could never carry. This explains why the majority decision in *Everson* contains perhaps the most sweeping ban on aid to religious schools ever used by the Court. One passage reads:

The "establishment of religion" clause of the First Amendment means at least this: Neither a state nor the Federal

Government can set up a church. Neither can pass laws which aid one religion, aid all religions, or prefer one religion over another. Neither can force nor influence a person to go to or remain away from church against his will or force him to profess a belief or disbelief in any religion. . . . No tax in any amount, large or small, can be levied to support any religious activities or institutions, whatever they may be called, or whatever form they may adopt to teach or practice religion.[4]

Nevertheless, the Court did concede the major point of the litigation to the Catholic schools. It did hold that use of public funds to provide transportation to these institutions did not violate the First Amendment. The result wrought near panic in some educational and church circles. Many leaders feared that Pandora's box had indeed been opened, that the camel's nose was now firmly in the tent. Despite the ringing assurance that the box was only to be opened a crack, and that everything but the nose was to be rigorously excluded, separationists felt a cold chill. This might well be the beginning of the end for church-state separation—an end that would be wrought by means of public subsidy to the schools of a church. Something had to be done about it.

Besides this, specific proposals were shortly advanced in Congress which would have channeled public aid to parochial schools. The Taft Bill strongly supported in 1948 originated a concept of school aid that would be much discussed in later years. Under its formula the Federal Government would make grants to the states which they would spend to improve education. This would mean that in states which permitted some use of public funds for parochial schools, the federal grants could be used for a similar purpose. In some states such aid was, in fact, being given to parochial schools in the matters of bus transportation and textbooks. Such a proposal would come as a welcome relief to many today, but strict separationists of that day saw in the Taft Bill and like proposals a kind of legislation which would erode separation of church and state. This was a trend to be resisted.

The initial Catholic reaction to the *Everson* decision was one of jubilation. Leaders of that church felt that they had now won bus transportation to their denominational schools. Many of them actually felt that the decision would have the effect of overriding inhibitions in state law and of enabling the parochial school bus at public expense everywhere. When they got to reading the fine print, however, they were not so happy. Some began to suspect that the Court had opened up the foyer only to slam shut the entrance to the auditorium. The bus decision did provide a wedge for Catholic action. While the decision specifically safeguarded the right of a state to provide transportation to public schools only, Catholic leaders frequently cited *Everson* as implying some kind of over-all justification for parochial buses at public expense everywhere.

Also, the Catholics used the "child benefit" concept of the *Everson* decision as one that could be widened to include other forms of aid. While government aid programs could not be used to benefit church schools they could be used to benefit the students in these schools on a health and welfare basis. With a little ingenuity and a bit of imagination, the child benefit theory could be stretched to include practically every phase of the parochial school program. Textbooks, for example, were common equipment for all school children and were of benefit to the child. Physical education had nothing to do with ideology but, rather, was for the child's physical development. Indeed, one could argue that most courses in the curriculum of the Catholic school had nothing to do with religion. Up to 90 per cent of the teaching program was secular training such as the state had intended to require under compulsory education laws. Why, therefore, could not the state pay up to 90 per cent of the instruction cost in Catholic schools without violating the establishment of religion clause of the First Amendment? As for buildings, it was certainly a matter of health and safety to have children educated in adequate and comfortable quarters. Catholic thinking along this line was climaxed by the statement of Father Virgil Blum, the Jesuit professor at Marquette University, who remarked that: "Education itself is one of these welfare benefits."[5]

Perhaps the Supreme Court itself had seen the possibility of mischief of this kind for it almost immediately sought to put a stopper in the leak which *Everson* had opened. In the following year, the Court accepted an Illinois case, *McCollum v. Board of Education*, and handed down the historic opinion that a program of religious instruction in public school classrooms and under public school discipline was unconstitutional.[6] This was so, the Court ruled, even though those who did not wish to take the course were free to go to another room and continue their secular studies. The Court held that this program violated the Constitution because compulsory education laws assisted and because the course offered was integrated with the system of religious instruction carried on by certain religious groups. The Court cited the *Everson* doctrine that government could not aid any or all religions in the dissemination of their doctrines.

The reaction of the Catholic hierarchy to the *McCollum* decision was one of outspoken opposition. Their opposition sprang from the fact that they saw in the Supreme Court's interpretation of the separation doctrine a final ban on public subsidy to Catholic education. They argued, in reply, that the establishment clause of the First Amendment banned only the establishment of one church as the official religion. Government was free to subsidize all churches on a nonpreferential basis and the First Amendment was never intended to interfere with this, they insisted. Any other interpretation was "entirely novel." The bishops then openly announced that they and their co-religionists would seek to change this doctrine of the Court.

The battle was thus openly joined between the "cooperationists" who sought at least some public subsidy for denominational instruction and the "separationists" who opposed any such use of public funds whatsoever. The battle has gone on for nearly 20 years with the gigantic Roman Catholic organization holding and pressing the former view and the tiny but rapidly growing organization, Protestants and Other Americans United for Separation of Church and State, as the principal protagonist of the other.

Some idea of the church-state problem in regard to federal aid to education as it existed in the 1940's can be derived from this observation in the Manifesto of Americans United[7] which was adopted on Nov. 20, 1947:

Action on (federal aid to public education) has been held up by the pressure of this church which demands that its parochial schools shall share with the public schools in any such federal appropriation in the amount proportional to the number of pupils in each school system.

The church referred to was the Roman Catholic Church. It is significant that the same complaint about the same church is being made two decades later. The situation is the same except that the pressures surrounding it have been intensified. A majority of United States citizens have become convinced that federal aid to education is a necessity. The Roman Catholic hierarchy headed by Cardinal Spellman of New York still blocks any general aid program for the schools unless Catholic denominational schools shall be included in it. The result today, as is customary in politics, is a compromise solution. Federal aid is given by awkward, behind the barn methods which provide aid to parochial schools in ways which are designed to evade the church-state issue. The aid provided in the Elementary and Secondary Education Act of 1965 is called aid to parochial school students rather than aid to parochial schools. This nod to the constitutional problem really was a distinction without a difference.

This was the issue which loomed large in 1947 and 1948 for the first time in a hundred years. Protestant and Jewish leaders and public educators who had known nothing but church-state separation and had assumed it would always be there, began to take alarm at this first experiment upon their liberties. The thing was serious and dangerous enough, it seemed, for the constant attention of a special, independent organization set up to do that and nothing else but that. This feeling sparked the organization of Protestants and Other Americans United for Separation of Church and State. It appeared to these concerned leaders that there was just commencing a church-state controversy which would continue for many years in the future. They wanted to be equipped to cope with it and a specialized agency seemed to be the answer.

There was yet another factor in the mounting church-state concern. This was the appointment by President Franklin D. Roosevelt of Myron C. Taylor, an Episcopalian layman, as his "personal representative" at the Vatican. The move was made suddenly and due to preoccupation with the war effort it did not receive the attention which it ordinarily would have drawn. From the very first, however, it was an irritant to inter-creedal relations. Protestants regarded Mr. Taylor as what in practical effect he was—a United States Ambassador to the Pope. This nod of favoritism toward the Roman Catholic Church aroused the resentment of Protestants and was viewed as a threat to separation of church and state.

The *Manifesto* of Americans United declared:

We are not deceived by the disguise under which the appointee to this ambassadorship was labeled as the President's personal ambassador. The Pope himself made it perfectly clear . . . that his presence at the Vatican marked a distinct departure from our Government's long established policy. We hold that this ambassadorship constitutes an interlocking of the functions of church and state which is contrary to the principle of their complete separation."

Pressures were already being exerted for the establishment of a permanent ambassadorship to the Holy See on the ground that Vatican City was a political state and that such a policy would be perfectly valid. These were the pressures which finally prevailed upon President Harry S. Truman, in 1951, to appoint General Mark W. Clark as ambassador to the State of Vatican City. Concern over this issue was a definite factor in the creation of Protestants and Other Americans United for Separation of Church and State. While the organization was to be concerned with many issues, these two were paramount: It would oppose use of public funds for religious schools, and it would oppose appointment of a United States Ambassador to the Vatican.

These were never quite Protestant-Catholic issues. Many Roman Catholics, especially those educated in public schools and possessed of some background in the evils of clericalism, were deeply opposed to their church's subsidy drive. Even as late as the 1950's an occasional Catholic priest or bishop would pronounce himself against public subsidies for parish schools. But by the 1960's the traditional Catholic view was winning out. Scenting the cultural prestige and dominance which would accrue to them through the subsidy, the clergy closed ranks. Protesting voices lapsed into silence—the silence of the ecumenical movement—while the hierarchy established its subsidy demands as the official Catholic position and attempted to use its constituents as a pressure bloc to achieve it. Protestants who originally presented a solid phalanx of opposition to the Catholic program began to divide even as Catholics became more united. An extremist view centering in the faculty of Union Theological Seminary, New York City, and to some extent in the National Council of Churches, began to advocate public assistance to religious schools of an auxiliary "health and welfare" nature. They did so from an alleged brotherhooder's desire to "ease religious tensions," never really understanding that they were helping to open up a far more serious religious controversy.

The controversy over aid to religious schools was a dramatic issue—perhaps the most dramatic—in a much larger context of concern. What inspired the founders of POAU was the fear of clericalism. Clericalism can be defined as the political use of religious influence by a church for the purpose of its own aggrandizement. The founders of Americans United knew clericalism. They had studied it closely and felt the brunt of it in Europe and Latin America. They knew all too well how oppressively it leaned upon other churches and upon the culture itself. They saw in the Jeffersonian doctrine of separation of church and state a way to deliverance from this plague. If religion could be kept free and voluntary, all the dangers of an oppressive church with its clerical manipulation of the secular power could be avoided. There should be no interlocking of the processes of church and state—that was the decisive thing.

This would be true, particularly, at the point of finance. All citizens would be free from the tax for religion. They would be spared the ignominy of having to pay for a religious propagation and instruction in which they did not believe, or even, for that matter, for their own.

In the First Amendment they believed they had found the

redemptive formula: free exercise without establishment. "Congress shall make no law respecting an establishment of religion or prohibiting the free exercise thereof." The churches had complete liberty to operate as free, voluntary societies. They could hold services, make converts, enroll members, take voluntary contributions, own property, erect buildings, even enjoy tax exemption. But government would not get into their business, would not provide any official promotion or opposition, would give them no official status and no tax support.

As the founders of Americans United saw it, the Catholic effort for public subsidy to its schools was merely a phase in its larger program of clerical domination. While it might plead for "justice to little children," or for the "rights of God-centered schools," its real objective was political preferment for an ecclesiastical organization. The school subsidy business was merely a means to an end. The end was to level the wall of church-state separation and to create some kind of religious Establishment. So the *Manifesto* written by Dr. Charles Clayton Morrison analyzed the situation:

> *The powerful church, unaccustomed in its own history and tradition to the American ideal of separation of church and state, but flourishing under the religious liberty provided by our form of government. . . . has committed itself in authoritative declarations and by positive acts to a policy plainly subversive of religious liberty as guaranteed by the Constitution. This church holds and maintains a theory of the relation of church and state which is incompatible with the American ideal. It makes no secret of its intention to secure for itself, if possible, a privileged position in the body politic. In pursuit of this policy it has already made such gains that the principle of separation of church and state is in peril of nullification by legislatures and courts, and by Federal, state and local administrations.*

The connection between the school subsidy drive and the larger cultural objectives of the church was delineated in the *Manifesto:*

> *One of the long-range purposes of this church is to secure total support for its extensive system of parochial schools from the public treasury. Its strategy in furtherance of the purpose is to fracture the constitutional principle at one point after another where the action can be minimized as trivial or disguised as falling within some other category than that of its ultimate intent.*

The *Manifesto* then went on to point out that such forms of assistance to religious schools as lunches, bus transportation, textbooks, etc. were merely a convenient approach to total public support for such schools.

The *Manifesto* made clear that it was neither pro-Protestant nor anti-Catholic. It declared:

It is no part of our purpose to propagandize for the Protestant faith or any other, nor to criticize or oppose the teaching or internal practices of the Roman Catholic Church, or any other. We have no connection or sympathy with any movement that is tinged with religious fanatacism. Our motivation arises solely from our patriotic and religious concern for the maintenance of the separation of church and state under the American form of government.

There was a sense, however, in which the main thrust of POAU was "anti-Catholic." It was the Catholic bishops who had declared war on the Supreme Court's doctrine of the First Amendment. It was these Catholic leaders who had formally declared their intention to break down separation of church and state at least insofar as public subsidy to church enterprise was concerned. It was Catholic lobbyists who were already at work in Congress and in the state capitals to breach the money line for the benefit of their institutions. It was the Catholic Church which operated over 90 per cent of the denominational schools for which public subsidy was sought. It was the Catholic Church which through its diocesan structure and its numerous religious orders operated an immense welfare program integrally related to the church itself, a program ideally constituted for partnership in the welfare state. It was, in fact, the Roman Catholic politicians who for 25 years had covertly worked to crumble the wall of separation by devising countless trickles of money to Roman Catholic institutions.

It is true that Americans United frequently found itself pitted against certain Protestant interests. It is true that we have incurred the wrath of a few Protestant boardsmen—denominational and institutional leaders—who feel that the time has come for "cooperation" between church and state and that Americans United is in the way. Some of these leaders fail to see the distinction between cooperation and capitulation. But all this is in a way shadow boxing. Protestant organizations really have no heart for public subsidy. They fear absorption in the welfare state as their institutions become financially dependent on government. Besides, all their predilections are against association with the state. Their traditions, training, background incline them otherwise. They have a feeling of guilt and shame over the use of public funds for their church enterprises.

Catholic leadership simply has none of this. Its tradition is different: it is steeped in centuries of association with the state. Its predilections are different: it has long been accustomed to the use of public funds. It has no fear that public funds will be followed by public controls. It has lived with this problem across the ages, and is confident of its ability to shape the state according to its own needs and ambitions.

The declared purpose of Americans United in its *Manifesto* won wide acclaim:

> *Its single and only purpose is to assure the maintenance of the American principle of separation of church and state upon which the Federal Constitution guarantees religious liberty to all the people and all churches of this Republic.*

Yet, in the furtherance of this purpose it soon became evident that Americans United would be involved increasingly in controversy with the Roman Church. This controversy was fought out, first, in the context of government aid to church institutions. This battle began to go against Americans United following the assassination of President Kennedy and particularly after the election of President Johnson in 1964. As we shall see, this battle was all but won for Catholic Action by an end run maneuver which sought to skirt the constitutional issue. In this maneuver much of the old-line Protestant leadership concurred and even participated.

It appeared that the controversy between the Catholic bishops and POAU would take a new turn in the late 1960's. POAU's role would be that of opposing clericalism. The Catholic bishops had shown considerable skill in using their constituency as a political power bloc to wring concessions from the Federal Government while at the same time bypassing, circumventing, or even overtly changing the constitutional provisions of the state which guaranteed church-state separation. As they have so often done in the past, there was every indication that these leaders would again go "too far." That is, they would follow up their brilliant success in the school aid battle with successive power thrusts for more and more preferment.

POAU was in the way of becoming an anticlerical force. It would be so not in the continental sense where anticlericalism had sometimes taken the shape of secularism or atheism. After all, much of its leadership was supplied by Protestant clergymen. Any anti-religious character for POAU would be out of the question. The organization would, rather, mount an educational and legal program seeking to inform the nation as to the perils of clericalism. As the big city politicians crumbled before the pressures of the church, as the welfare alliance of church and state became more intimate, as the scope of church tax-exempt property and business continued to burgeon, Americans United would register its dissent. The case is not so hopeless as it might appear. History records many an instance when the pendulum swung the other way.

[1] *Church and State in the United States*, Stokes & Pfeffer, Harper & Row, New York City (1964), page 232.

[2] House Committee on Education and Labor on Federal Aid to Education, 1947, pages 310, 311.

[3] Statement of the Catholic Bishops of the United States, November 21, 1948, published by the National Catholic Welfare Conference.

[4] *Everson, People ex rel v. Board of Education*, 330 U. S. 1 333 U. S. 201.

[5] *U. S. News & World Report*, October 25, 1957, page 109.

[6] 333 U.S. 203 (1948).

[7] For the sake of brevity, I shall use the shorter form of the name—POAU or Americans United.

Glenn L. Archer with Mrs. Willie L. Blum, first employee of Americans United. Photo was taken in 1948.

chapter **II** **THE MAN**

A facility for management is part of the native endowment of Glenn Leroy Archer. He has always been running things. When his father died suddenly at the age of 60, it was Glenn Archer who picked up the reins of management and saved the sprawling enterprises from bankruptcy. The farms his father had acquired were manned by tenants who had gone ten years without a crop. Garfield Joseph Archer died with the end of the dust bowl era just ahead but not yet in sight. If one could hold on, there might be hope. But holding on was a problem. All the farms, together with the lumber yard, the grain elevator, and other enterprises were mortgaged to the hilt. There were interest payments to be met. The bank was ready to take over.

His son, Glenn, took over instead. It was not merely a labor of love; it was a point of pride. He refused to accept the possibility that his father's ventures should come to bankruptcy. This was not going to happen and he would personally see to it. One day, Garfield Joseph Archer looked out across the fields and said: "The saints of God shall conquer though they die." Then he collapsed in his chair and died. Such an incident challenges credulity. The fact that a businessman should have been thinking about the saints of God seems chimerical. Yet this man only died as he had lived. Garfield Joseph Archer never took a vacation. He never "wasted time" in social life. When his son, Glenn, served a four-year term as secretary to the Governor of Kansas he called on him in the capitol just once. He came to the son's home for Thanksgiving dinner when the amenities called for it, paid his respects when the meal was over and went to his office. There was no time for idleness or frivolity. When there was business to be discussed he drove to the son's house, sounded the horn and, when the son emerged, they would discuss matters. There was no fooling around. It was all right to the point.

As chairman of the trustees of Central College, McPherson, Kansas, 37 years Sunday School superintendent of the local church, and as a Kansas State legislator, Garfield Joseph Archer brought the same powers of concentration to bear. He managed church business or public business exactly as he managed his own. He was incessantly diligent. His life is incomprehensible apart from his religion. He was a man spiritually motivated in business. His prudence was spurred by godliness. He was not Calvinist in his beliefs but he had the Calvinist drive to "prove one's calling." How did one live the Christian life? By attending church services, assuming one's responsibilities there, by doing good to one's neighbor as one found opportunity—but also by diligence in business. The Christian could not be irresponsible or careless in such matters. He must be punctilious for in this he was being what God expected of him.

This was the mantle which fell upon the son in 1940. The immediate and tangible responsibility was for the various business enterprises of the elder Archer which, because of the "cropless decade" of the thirties, were in precarious situation. Many had simply packed up and left. It is typical of the Archers that they never budged. Apparently, they never considered budging. They were a part of Kansas for good or ill. They were there to fight the thing through. It was nip-and-tuck for Glenn Archer. But the rains began to fall again and the dust bowl began to come back. Along with the heavy responsibilities that he was carrying at the time, Glenn Archer managed his father's estate on the side. He saw to it that his brother and sister finished college. He provided for his mother. He paid off the debts which had accumulated. He held every one of the heavily mortgaged properties and firmly paid them off, one by one.

At the height of this activity he was also serving as secretary to Governor Payne Ratner of Kansas. Then came dual responsibilities as director of public relations for the Kansas Teachers Association and as associate director of the Legislative Division and Federal Relations of the National Education Association. He could carry on multiple activities efficiently because he had built-in capacity. All through school, he was regularly president of his class, honor student, captain of the teams, editor of the annual and the school paper. It was his practice to win all the honors and scholarships that were available.

THE MAN

At Greenville College, age 19, Glenn Archer was named dean of men and became proctor of 150 boys. It is characteristic of him that he should have felt the weight of his responsibilities so seriously that he decided not to do any dating. This might appear frivolous and undermine discipline. The decision was rendered easier by the fact that he had already fallen in love with Ruth Agnes Ford at the age of 13. Having decided that this was the girl he wanted to marry, he pursued this goal with the same dedication that he devoted to all others. He reports that while he supposes that he was attracted to other girls from time to time during the next eight years, there was never any serious diversion from his main line interest. At the age of 21 he married Ruth. Today, she is not only his wife, she is his secretary and one of the quickest and most capable to be found anywhere.

Many of the achievements of Glenn Archer have come as by-products of his voracious appetite for excellence which devoured everything within reach. Elected editor of the Greenville College *Papyrus*, he decided that he ought to learn something about journalism. He duly enrolled in a summer course at the University of Iowa where he was named night editor of the *Daily Iowan*. He found time to pitch the School of Journalism to the summer school baseball championship, a distinction it had not previously achieved. When he assumed direction of the *Papyrus* he promptly named his defeated rival for the honor to be his assistant. This was done because "he was the best writer on the campus."

Glenn L. Archer became a lawyer as a result of a similar fortuity. He had been serving as associate to the Legislative Division and Federal Relations of the NEA and at the same time as director of public relations for the Kansas State Teachers' Association. It was wartime and he was about to be called by his draft board. He returned to Kansas to await the call which was expected momentarily. When the call did not develop as soon as he had anticipated, he decided to sign up for a four weeks law course at Washburn University in Topeka and hope that he could complete it. He did complete it. There was to be a further six weeks delay in his draft call. He signed up for six weeks additional courses at the law school. Then yet another six weeks. Finally, Glenn Archer completed the 27 months law course in about half the regular time and graduated *magna cum laude* with the highest grades in the history of the school. He had won all the scholarships available and was offered the deanship at the end of his first year's work, upon the condition he would go on to graduation.

When he returned to Washington, D.C., upon graduation from law school, he was again offered the job as head of the NEA's legislative division. But the deanship at Washburn had more appeal. Friends on the inside had given him to know that he could go from the deanship to a place on the Kansas Supreme Court and that there would be support for him to seek the Republican nomination for Governor. It was a rosy path leading step-by-step to a career of honor and distinction. There could be slips, of course. No one ever knows about politics. But barring any of those unforeseen developments that can upset the best apple carts, this man had it made. He had the experience, the friends, the support, the money to go all the way in his native state.

The apple cart was upset. Something drastic happened to change the entire course of events into which Glenn L. Archer had comfortably settled himself. There was a juxtaposition of man and event that pulled this life off into another orbit altogether. He was to be one of the best hated and best loved men of his generation.

When this thing happened it could not have happened to a man better equipped for it. Glenn Archer has the most prodigious memory I have ever encountered. It is not a memory for this or for that; it is a memory for everything. Women are famous for their powers of recollection when these are addressed to the frock Aunt Nellie wore at the Smith's party in 1940. Glenn Archer has this same kind of retention. Many a time I have witnessed a phone call from somebody who met him at Pocatello, Idaho in 1950. He will instantly focus the entire event, recall who introduced him, how many were at the meeting, and what the man had said to him afterward on the way to the plane. He never forgets anything, whether important or trivial.

His memory for names is peculiar. He can always come up with a piece of it on the first try. Then he will fumble with it, turn it over and around, and finally develop the correct handle. He seems to have thousands of names stored away in this truncated condition, ready to be brought out and rehabilitated as needed. He has phenomenal retentive powers in regard to conversations, the most trivial observations of board members and even the facial expressions which accompanied them. He has never had to be a great trouble-shooter with his organization. He has had, rather, the facility of recognizing trouble in its embryo state, long before it came to birth. At the hint of trouble he was off to its lair, treating it as it needed to be treated, scotching it before it had a chance to grow and get somewhere. He has always assumed that even his closest friends among the directors might detect something wrong in his management and cherish a grievance in regard to it. He has insisted on facing up to everything immediately, even though it turned out to be something that was not there.

Numbers, though, are the Archer specialty. He can remember every number that crossed his threshold or even rapped on the door. He can tell you what he paid for a suit or a bushel of corn in 1932. He can give you the budget of Americans United for every year of its existence, will tell you with pride that they made it every year and what the margin was. This was usually pretty close, by the way, but never once was there a finish in the red. Archer saw to that.

One of his finest arts is that of keeping people who are angry from getting too angry. This has been a useful grace in dealing with a few the boardsmen and connectional leaders of the churches. Americans United has been constantly drawing the censure of a few of these leaders. They might unthinkingly fall into the cliche adroitly developed and spread by the National Catholic Welfare Conference that the organization was "bigoted" and "anti-Catholic" because it opposed Catholic ambitions for tax support. Or, they might be resentful of the group because of its staff and the range of its operations which tended to dwarf their own. Or, they might be angry because Americans United seemed to be getting so much attention when they knew perfectly well that they, and only they, were properly credentialed to speak for Protestants. Or, they might be just plain angry because exposure by the organization prevented their obtaining some juicy federal patronage. Impervious to epithets and recriminations, Glenn Archer patiently deals with angry men. His soft answers have turned away more wrath than the scripture writer could possibly have had in mind. He speaks softly and carries only a small stick. He can get violently angry, but never over anything important. He knows that he cannot afford the luxury of such a lapse and does not permit it.

Archer has had basically two kinds of critics to handle—those who think he is too hard on the Catholic Church and those who think he is not nearly hard enough. He has threaded a tortuous middle ground between the two for 19 years, losing some of the professional brotherhooders on the one extreme and the rabid rabids on the other. But all the while he has kept in motion a steadily growing, hard-hitting apparatus which has consistently and intelligently opposed America's rising tide of clericalism.

He has a way of disarming a critic that will work unless the man is just plain bigoted and beyond reprieve. I have seen some of his most violent critics transformed into avid supporters by the Archer treatment. I have tried to analyze it, tried to imitate it, without results. The key to it, I think, is to consummate disinterestedness as to his own importance. He is quite capable of standing off to the side and viewing his own capacities with an unbiased eye. When a critic scathingly identifies Archer's limitations he will cooly agree without the slightest loss of self respect. He will state factually that he has always had serious reservations about his ability to lead such a movement but that now in it and committed to it as he is, he knows he needs all the help he can get. An irreverent member of the staff has referred to this as "Archer's poor boy treatment." What makes it work is that he means it.

Glenn Archer came from the farm. He acknowledges it with joy and pride. His conversation is salted with homely parables and aphorisms which often have the touch of the land:

"He's a good man in the parlor but no good in the kitchen."

"He can't plow a straight furrow."

"It's one thing to have a frame; its another thing to put a painting in the frame."

"It's better to have somebody you have to pull in than somebody you have to kick off the chair."

"I put the harness on you just as fast as I could without creating sores."

"The trouble with us is that we are bringing people to dinner but not feeding them anything."

"You make the call. That will leave a card free to roam the deck."

"He's like the sparks off the anvil but lacks the steady heat to melt anything."

"I'm trying to keep the team together without upsetting the buggy."

"We have different foods for different appetites."

"You can't fight fire with a dead torch."

"He operates like two wagon wheels in three ruts."

"He's having a 14-pound child with a six-pound pair of hips."

"He's like a plow that starts out digging 12 inches. Then, the first thing you know, it's only three inches."

"When we cut him down the woods didn't miss him."

"We will use him as a broom to sweep away a few cobwebs."

"When you reply to critics like him you are watering a pumpkin vine."

"He says there are difficulties. Is that bad? If Lincoln had had his way paid, and no problems, he'd have ended up as a pot-bellied tavern keeper in Chicago."

"It seems like I know more people in the cemetery than I do in town."

I have heard him use hundreds of these and I have never heard him repeat. He has a different one for each occasion and the one he uses is just right.

Being from the farm Glenn Archer is rather fond of the diamond-in-the-rough stance. He likes to pretend that he has no social graces, is embarrassed in company and does not know what to do with his feet. He will convulse an audience with an account of some social gaucherie. There is a little truth in this. He does not really care for social life. Like his father, he considers it a waste of time. But he can turn it on when he needs it. No man can be so gracious, so quick with the correct pleasantry. He can charm one person, a room full or an audience of many thousands. He may be sweating over it but this does not appear. He does it with the ease of a man born to the drawing room and the light fantastic. He can do what he wants to do, what he needs to do.

Glenn Archer is an orator. We don't have these any more. They went out with William Jennings Bryan. He lacks the tremendous organ voice that Bryan used to entrance 20,000 hearers without a microphone. But he has Bryan's "rousement." He is about the only speaker I know in America today who can come to the end of his address with people standing in the aisles yelling like Indians, bringing him back for one encore after another like an opera diva. When he is right he will sweep the deck—any deck you put him on.

In 1956 at the Southern Baptist Convention in Kansas City before an audience of 8,000, he swept into the following peroration which concluded his address:

Separation of church and state is basic to spirituality—a spirituality without which religion is dead and formal. The future of America depends not upon a state religion but upon a religion that is real, vital, deep and spiritual. A personal experience which enables one to attune with the eternal, and thus achieve life's noblest estate, a man made in the image of God. A rich estate which neither government nor state church can will or bequeath. God alone can make man Godlike.

The simulated "demonstrations" which accompany nominating speeches at political conventions were drab compared with what followed. The audience sent up a mighty roar of approval and applause, bringing the speaker back to the rostrum time after time. One veteran observer called it "the greatest demonstration for a speaker" that he had seen in 50 years attendance at church conventions.

If he is on the program of a church conference or convention Glenn Archer will invariably have the largest audience, draw the most applause, and send the audience away cheering loudly or muttering imprecations. He makes an impact on the people who hear him. He has, too, an uncanny knack of adjusting to the audience, an art that has become vestigial in an age of canned speeches. I have seen him start out on a line to which an audience did not appear responsive, then quickly shift gears and move on to another track. He would end up with the audience in his pocket. I have never seen him fail in a speech and I have heard him speak on many occasions. Again, this is something he will not permit. He will keep working and experimenting until he finds the formula he needs. Then he will lift them out of their seats. He is a musician who plays the audience like an instrument. This is not rabble-rousing; it is getting through to the people wherever they are. Glenn Archer can get through. In this respect—and what else would come ahead of it? —he is one of the ablest platform speakers in America today.

Perhaps the most basic description of the man is in the observation that he represents a complete union of thought and action. He has a sublime impatience with purely theoretical study or discussion. In his mind ideas are never separated from the means of putting them into effect. It is no use to discuss a new building unless you consider how to raise the money. It is futile to talk grandiloquently of a great national program to save separation of church and state apart from the problem of ways and means of doing it. Whatever has worth is worth doing.

People are always marveling at the ubiquity of Americans United. That outfit keeps popping up everywhere. Its hand appears in one controversy after another from coast to coast and lakes to gulf. It even reaches its long arm abroad straightening people out on the subject of religious freedom wherever problems are to be found. How can the group do so much for so many? Partially, at least, because its staff members do not spend their time sitting around in theoretical discussions. The time and energy consumed by others in considering what ought to be done is expended by Americans United in doing it. That is just the trouble, its critics say. These people are always rushing in. They do hastily and inadequately what we could do so much better if we ever got around to it.

There is some merit in these objections. Perhaps there is a dearth of theory and of ideological discussion at Americans United. "Let's get to the point," is a typical Archerism. The point is always what we can do and how we can do it. The *modus operandi* he taught us is really very simple. What we fundamentally do is to fight expenditures of public funds for churches. Wherever and whenever such expenditures are proposed, we oppose them. We appeal to the pride and tradition of free churchmen. We appeal to legislators to draft their laws with strict separation in mind. We go to the theater of public opinion in press and other mass media. We go to the courts. We publish and distribute literature. We lecture, preach, and educate that there is something destructive and evil about church institutions receiving subsidies from the state. Under the Glenn Archer leadership we have not only proclaimed this we have everlastingly been doing something about it. This wedding of the idea and action in the organization is the direct infusion of the man. We have done what he is.

Americans United could well have been another of those good, gray groups—noble, musty and innocuous—conducting studies for the edification of owlish specialists. Despite the belittling language, these groups do have a place and, in the long run, do wield influence. But Americans United is not of this breed. It is a do-it-yourself-now group. The reason the organization has grown and flourished for 19 years is the realization of this fact by its members and donors. They know that they can get more action per dollar out of Americans United than they can anywhere else.

Put it this way—in Glenn Archer the thought and the deed are perfectly blended so that for him to think on some useful and productive course of action is tantamount to starting in on it. This does not mean he starts in on everything. He starts on only those projects which he feels he has the means to complete. But when he has thought a thing through and committed himself to it, he will pursue his goal with a terrible determination.

He is a man of so many facets that it is hard to pick the one most notable. I think it was his business acumen that impressed me most. Probably since I have none of this myself. He could do more with less than any man I ever met. Doing more with less is a kind of religion with him. To waste a dollar is to commit a sin. I have already alluded to his memory for figures. It is not merely a matter of memory. Archer thinks financial. When he goes into a restaurant he will begin making a mental note of how many the place can seat, the probable rent, labor cost and other overhead. Then after a look at the menu he will rapidly calculate how many meals they must sell per day in order to turn a profit. When he enters a hotel he may run through a similar calculation based on the number of rooms and the rates leading him to a conclusion as to the rate of occupancy that the place would need. He took an ugly, abandoned, worn out farm in West Virginia and, in spare moments, turned it into a place of beauty and income.

Glenn Archer thinks of every problem not only in terms of the problem itself, as an academic matter, but also in terms of the money it would take to do something about it. He recognizes that everything one faces has its money aspect. It is not that only, but it is that partially. Until one gets that phase of it into view he has not seen the whole matter. This "money sense" of the director has made Americans United an amazing success story. The organization has made its budget every year, undertaken only such projects as it could finance, and has conspicuously avoided the rock of fiscal irresponsibility on which many nonprofit groups have foundered. Lloyd Leidig, a banker in Lenora, Kansas, who has had ample opportunity to know, once described Glenn L. Archer as "the best customer I ever had in my 60 years of banking."

There is yet another characteristic of Archer which deserves comment. He is inexorable in dealing with himself. One must always do and be one's very best. This feeling for perfection can be seen in his reading habits. It is amazing that he would have time to read at all. Harassed and driven as he has been all his life, with his home almost as much an office as 1633 Massachusetts Avenue, it would seem reasonable to suppose that all his waking hours would be occupied with Americans United. It always seemed so to his associates. Yet, amazingly, he is a steady reader, if not a prodigious one. Characteristically, he never reads anything but the best. I shall never forget his look of disdain when someone remarked that he read detective stories to put himself to sleep. Archer remarked that Tolstoy would serve the same purpose.

Archer reads Victor Hugo, Dickens, Thackeray, Stevenson and Dostoevski, He is an avid student of *War and Peace* and *The Brothers Karamazov*. He read *Doctor Zhivago* with close attention and was prepared to discuss whether the Russian high command had been justified in condemning the book. He read Faulkner not, I think, because he liked him, but because Faulkner was a serious writer and deserved attention. He has a good grasp of Shakespeare and Shaw. He has an excellent layman's knowledge of the Bible. Whatever comes up, if it is in the field of the classics, he is familiar with it and prepared to advance his views about it. "I don't read a lot of books," he wryly remarks, "but I reread a lot of good books."

It is as a physical culturist perhaps that we get our most graphic impression of the man. His basement is filled with all kinds of equipment for physical exercise—weights, bars, springs, pulleys, etc. He has two sessions of exercise every day, plus a bicycle ride or walk. He maintains this practice whether he is at home or on the road, always rising at 6 A.M. to have plenty of time. He believes that muscles are meant to be used. I have seen him do 70 pushups in the office just to clear his head. He can do 100 pushups without stopping and I have seen him do it. Horseback riding is one of his passions. Once when he was 58 years old a stirrup strap gave way and tossed him skyward from his horse. He recalled his tumbling and rolling to a stop without injury. He got to his feet, remounted the animal and completed a five mile ride. The man has arms like trees. His entire body is solid as flint. Someone has remarked that Archer's passion for physical fitness is "compulsive." I suppose it is. But then, most things about him are compulsive. He has that overriding sense of duty. We are here to work. What is expected of a man is the very best of which he is capable.

When Archer graduated from college he believed himself to be called to the mission field. He presented himself to the board prepared for an assignment abroad. These were the depression years. The board was calling missionaries home, not sending out new ones. Archer was turned down and the board lost a tremendous missionary. When we consider him as a frustrated missionary, this may be an authentic angle.

What we see in Archer and Americans United is a fortuitous blending of a man and a cause which makes an impact on society. For this to happen there has to be something more than the cause—there has to be a man like Glenn Archer. They don't often happen like him.

Men used to believe and feel strongly about it. Men would bob up here and there who believed that God meant for them to do some specific things. There was no foolishness about this. They really believed it. Their life became a kind of debt which they had to pay off. They went about it as men indentured to God. Call it fanatacism, call it anything you will, but it is a fact.

This gift for believing and doing is well knocked by people who are incapable of either. It is safe to say that a majority of those living today simply cannot understand a man like Glenn L. Archer or a movement like Protestants and Other Americans United for Separation of Church and State. Both are really a throwback to a former time. Part of it, most of it, was religion. It was the feeling for God that dug into such people. This feeling—and what else but feeling impels men?—has vanished from the major Protestant churches today. With their extensive bureaucracies almost rivaling that of government, their swollen treasuries, their vast memberships of the undisciplined and the uncommitted, they are too much in general to be anything in particular. There is neither opportunity nor occasion for individuals to rise up with a mission.

But this can and does happen in the sects. Here believers can believe something. They are capable of not being careful. They can throw caution to the winds. They can behave as though some things really matter and God cares about them. They can commit. For vestigial survivals of this spirit today one must look to the sects. Many of the staff leaders of Americans United have roots in the sects. You can take the man out of the sect but you can't take the sect out of the man. Glenn L. Archer was born and bred not a Methodist which he is today, but a Free Methodist which he still is in heart. I am a product of the Christian and Missionary Alliance and remember this with gratitude, though today I am a loyal minister of the Methodist Church. Gioele Settembrini, a Southern Baptist, has Waldensian origins. W. Phillips Berwick, regional director in Chicago, is a Methodist minister with a background in the Mennonite Brethren in Christ and Church of God. Others who have served Americans United have been products of the sects.

To do what Glenn Archer has done a man would have to be a little bit "crazy." That is, he would have to set aside and repudiate those ends which men today conventionally seek. He would have to decide that money was not too important a commodity and that material possessions did not really come first. Having reached such a conclusion Archer would already be set off in a slim ten per cent or less of the thinking population. Then when he decided, as he did decide, that a particular cause was his and that he should give everything he had to it, that would put him practically alone. They don't make them like this any more.

Perhaps such a man could come only from a spot like Densmore, Kansas where Glenn Leroy Archer was born in 1906. Kansas is no bargain at best. During the dust bowl epoch it was even worse than ever. One had to shake the dust out of the sheets before going to bed. In the desperate thirties there were circles around the sun and the atmosphere wore a creeping yellow hue. The dust one breathed was the Kansas topsoil gone with the wind. Add to these the regular scourges of the place. Kansas is flat. It is bitter cold in the winter and blazing hot in the summer. No: Kansas is no bargain. Yet there are those who love it. Glenn Archer is never so eloquent as when he speaks of his native state. Its drab, treeless terrain, its monotonous flatland, its difficult soil with meager return, can stir him to heights of nostalgic enthusiasm.

The Archer roots in Kansas were strong and deep. A wealth of family tradition can create its own beauty. Glenn Archer's paternal grandfather, Cyrus Archer and his wife Elizabeth Bates Archer, homesteaded in the Solomon River Valley, laid out and named the town of Densmore, built the first church, dug the first grave in the local cemetery which was on land they donated. Cyrus Archer had five brothers and two sisters who soon followed him to Kansas. All brought young brides or husbands, homesteaded, and reared their families in the valley. Grandmother and Grandfather Archer reared to adulthood eight of their twelve children. All eight became ministers of the Gospel. At one time in the local church there were 325 members and the records showed that 270 of them were either Archers or married to Archers. Quite a tradition for a man to have back of him.

But what of the terrain? Is there a connection between where a man was born and what he is? We know that tender plants have at times sprung from dry ground. Palestine is the land of the prophets. No other land can remotely rival the steady procession of spiritual giants that have emerged there. Amos, Hosea, Isaiah, Jeremiah, Paul, John were all its products. But what a sorry land it is! What a wretched, barren place. How could any good thing come from it?

Perhaps it is more than chance or fluke that the leader of one of the few authentic movements in this century in the United States should have come from unpromising soil where life was hard and toil was not always requited. Anyway, this was the soil and the heritage from which Glenn Archer came to be executive director of Protestants and Other Americans United for Separation of Church and State.

Leo Pfeffer, counsel for the American Jewish Congress and Elder Charles S. Longacre of the Department of Religious Liberty, Seventh Day Adventist Church (left and right, respectively), receive the 1956 Religious Liberty Citations from Glenn L. Archer (center) executive director of Americans United.

Rev. Charles L. Hoch, Rev. John L. Gregory, Dr. Eugene Carson Blake, stated clerk of the Presbyterian Church, U.S.A., Gov. Joseph B. Johnson of Vermont, Dr. Glenn L. Archer, executive director of Americans United, and Rev. Harry C. Ford at a Council of Churches meeting, Montpelier, Vt., Nov. 4, 1956.

The Founders: Dr. Charles Clayton Morrison, Dr. Edwin McNeill Poteat, Bishop G. Bromley Oxnam, Glenn L. Archer, Dr. Joseph Martin Dawson, at the annual board meeting of Americans United in 1949.

chapter III MAN AND EVENT UNITE

The acceptance of Glenn L. Archer of the post as executive director of Americans United in July of 1948 was of decisive importance in the life of the organization. When he came there really was nothing to come to. It had no budget, no building, no equipment, no staff. It was nothing but an idea. It was no more than an idea for there was no draft or blueprint for organization, no plan by which POAU could be built into the national structure its founders envisaged. The founders were convenors who thought up the idea, prepared the *Manifesto*, persuaded Archer to take the job, then left it up to him.

The founders were busy men. They had their own responsibilities to carry. It is everlasting to their credit that they saw the need and were willing to put as much time and effort into forming the new group as they did. Most of them stayed right with Protestants and Other Americans United for Separation of Church and State and were willing consultants through the years, up to their retirement and beyond. But the building and the management of Americans United, the day-to-day operation, and above all the financial responsibility—all rested squarely on the shoulders of Glenn L. Archer from the day he became director.

The founders were a curious combination of liberals and fundamentalists, of Council of Churches and national and fraternal leaders. Clergymen were prominent in the deliberations. It was such a combination as might not have desired to be caught together under any other possible set of circumstances. But to defend separation of church and state they did come together. Perhaps the most interesting development of all was the inclusion of "loners"—groups well known for pursuing their own course in their own way. Seventh-day Adventists and Christian Scientists were active in the formation of Americans United, were generous in supplying leadership and support. There were Jews among the original organizers and they have always remained active in leadership. The Jewish community at large, however, has always held aloof from Americans United. The explanation offered was that the name was not suitable— Protestants and Other Americans United for Separation of Church and State. This, many of them explained, appeared to make Jews second class members. They could not be mollified by the practical adoption of the shorter form, Americans United, which soon came into general use. But fundamentally Jewish groups are hesitant to get in any cross-fire that might be considered, even falsely, religious.

Who were the persons responsible for Americans United? Perhaps the first to be mentioned was one who did not live to see its consumation. Dr. Rufus W. Weaver, a prominent Baptist leader and former president of Mercer University, who was living in Washington, D.C. during the 1940's, was the first to see the necessity of such a group. He was impressed with the amazing gap in the thinking of politicians in matters relating to church and state. They were, most of them, simply not aware of the separation tradition. He foresaw that while Baptists generally might be more alert on the subject than others, it was too much to expect that Baptists alone could lead the kind of effort needed to preserve church-state separation. This thinking Dr. Weaver shared with Dr. Joseph Martin Dawson who in 1946 had assumed his post in Washington as the first executive director of the Baptist Joint Committee on Public Affairs. Elder C. S. Longacre, Seventh-day Adventist leader, was also groping for some kind of denominational cooperation to preserve religious liberty.

On September 19, 1946, at the call of Dr. Weaver, a number of persons gathered at the Carroll Arms Hotel in Washington, D.C. to discuss the need for cooperative action in the church-state field. One of those present at this meeting was Senator Olin Johnston of South Carolina. On February 5, 1947, following the death of Dr. Weaver, a group convened in Washington at the Wardman Park Hotel to discuss the matter further. Present on this occasion were Dr. Charl Ormond Williams, president of the National Education Association; Editor Elmer E. Rogers of the Scottish Rite magazine, *The New Age;* Editor H. H. Votaw of the Seventh-day Adventist Religious Liberty Department;

Dr. Clyde W. Taylor, secretary of the National Association of Evangelicals; Dr. Frank B. Gigliotti, a Presbyterian minister prominent in civic affairs; Elder C. S. Longacre, and several others. Presiding at the gathering was Dr. J. M. Dawson.

There were other meetings with additional members joining the group. There was one at the National Memorial Baptist Church in Washington on May 15, 1947, another at Calvary Baptist Church there on October 18 of the same year, the latter under the presidency of Methodist Bishop G. Bromley Oxnam. The climactic meeting was held at the Chicago Methodist Temple, November 20, 1947, with an invitation to all who supported separation of church and state. On the evening of November 19, Dr. Charles Clayton Morrison, editor of *The Christian Century,* sought the consultation of Dr. Dawson in regard to a *Manifesto* which he had been invited to prepare for the new organization. He and Dr. Dawson sat up most of the night going over the document line by line. The *Manifesto* was further analyzed by the full meeting composed of more than 60 persons. Eventually the *Manifesto* was endorsed with enthusiasm as the *raison d'etre* of Protestants and Other Americans United for Separation of Church and State. It was released to the press which hailed it for the significant document it was. *The New York Times* printed the full text and many other newspapers throughout the United States gave it copious attention.

Officers selected by the group were: president, Edwin McNeill Poteat, president of Colgate-Rochester Divinity School; first vice president, Charles Clayton Morrison, editor of *The Christian Century;* second vice president, John A. Mackay, president of Princeton Theological Seminary and former moderator of the Presbyterian Church, U.S.A.; third vice president, Louie D. Newton, president of the Southern Baptist Convention; secretary, J. M. Dawson, executive director of the Baptist Joint Committee on Public Affairs; treasurer, E. J. DeGroot, Jr. of Washington, D. C., attorney. On January 29, 1948 a charter was granted to Protestants and Other Americans United for Separation of Church and State under the laws of the District of Columbia.

To emphasize the stature of the founding leadership of POAU it can be pointed out that its board of trustees included men who were currently holding, or would soon hold, the highest elective offices in America's three largest Protestant denominations—Southern Baptist, Methodist, and Presbyterian. There were others of comparable stature.

In order to have some kind of interim operation until a full time director could be named, Dr. J. M. Dawson consented to serve as acting executive of POAU. A committee headed by Dr. Charl Ormond Williams was named to search for the right man to be named director. The committee agreed that he must be a man of unimpeachable character, of definite convictions, discreet and sincere, experienced in public relations, and completely dedicated to the group's announced objectives. Many persons were considered and a number interviewed. Dr. Williams herself eventually came up with the name which all agreed upon. She had observed during her long tenure with the NEA the work of an incisive young man who knew how to get things done. She had watched him in action and realized at once that he was a winner. She advanced the name of Glenn L. Archer, dean of the Washburn University Law School, Topeka, Kansas.

Glenn L. Archer was meticulously checked. Everybody who knew him when and then was consulted. Former Kansas Governor Payne H. Ratner whom Archer had so capably served as executive secretary, former Kansas Governor Alfred M. Landon, the Republican presidential nominee in 1932, Archer's Topeka law partners, his associates in the NEA, his bishops, and many others—all agreed that there could be no better man to direct the operations of Americans United. But there remained the business of persuading Archer that this was the place for him.

On May 24, 1948 Glenn L. Archer flew to Washington to attend the convention of the American Law Institute. While at the hotel desk registering he heard his name on the loud speaker. On the telephone was Dr. J. M. Dawson who said: "Mr. Archer, I want very much to see you." Archer had never heard of J. M. Dawson, supposed at first that it must be his friend Dr. Howard A. Dawson of the NEA. But on getting the thing straight, Archer replied that his only opportunity to see Dr. Dawson would be that very day since he would be in sessions the rest of the week. At Dr. Dawson's request he took a taxi to the headquarters of the Baptist Joint Committee, climbed four flights of steps and met the Baptist executive for the first time.

Dr. Dawson explained about the new organization that had been formed and handed him a copy of the *Manifesto*. He read the names of the founders. Some of these were familiar to Archer. Then Dr. Dawson said abruptly: "What do you think of the idea?" Archer struggled for a reply. He said that he thought it might be a very good idea, that it was certainly in accord with his own belief in church-state separation. Archer relates it never occurred to him that Dawson was taking his measure as a possible executive director for the organization.

He flew back to Topeka and resumed his duties as dean of the Law School. Early in June, 1948 he was invited to return to Washington to meet the executive committee of Americans United with a view to the possibility of his becoming executive head of the new organization. He went out of curiosity but without any real intention of leaving his pleasant associations in Topeka.

Archer met for the first time Dr. Charles Clayton Morrison who with Dr. Dawson was to have a decisive influence in his life. These two interviewed Archer prior to the meeting of the executive committee and informed him that his was the name, and the only name, that would be submitted to the group next day as the nominee for executive director. At this direct confrontation Archer replied directly that he was not available. He pointed to his obligations in Kansas. They were personal, professional and business and were of such nature that the assumption of such a post in Washington would be out of the question. At their urging he did consent, however, to appear before the full committee next day.

As his name came under discussion Archer started to leave the room but was restrained by Dr. Morrison who then proceeded to put his name in nomination in highly laudatory terms. Archer recalls that Clyde W. Taylor of the NAE, later to be one of his closest associates, lifted his 6-foot-5 frame from his seat and, not realizing Archer was in the room, said: "All of this sounds good, but who is this Archer? Frankly, I have never heard of him. I certainly think we should have a chance to look at him before we vote."

Dr. Taylor was startled when Glenn L. Archer, at the invitation of Dr. Morrison, rose from his place immediately behind the NAE executive and made his way to the front of the room. In his response to Dr. Morrison, Archer warmly thanked the committee for its kindness. He pointed out that he had presented himself for missionary service in the church following graduation from college but that due to the depression no candidates were being accepted. He had, he said, turned to teaching as an alternative form of service. He then went on to say:

It would be a rare privilege to be associated with you. But the real facts are that I am under a contract which does not expire for two years, and I simply could not break that contract and be worthy of the confidence that the University has conferred upon me. In addition, father died in 1940 and I am the only one of the family available to care for mother and her business concerns. I have law partners who rely upon me. Under these circumstances I see no way to leave Kansas at the present time. Nevertheless, I want to thank you for your approval and to assure you that I will do what I can to support financially this worthy cause, and to help its activities in my native state."

That did not end the matter; it only whetted the committee's appetite for the young Kansan. Dr. Taylor turned and gave Archer an approving smile. Elmer E. Rogers arose and said: "Mr. President, I suggest we give Mr. Archer time to consider this invitation further. I am convinced that we have nominated the right man and that we may yet persuade him to accept." E. H. DeGroot also spoke a word of commendation. Louie D. Newton, pastor of the great Druid Hills Baptist Church in Atlanta, came to Archer and said: "Mr. Archer, I hope you will reconsider this matter. If you will take this job, I will stand by you to the end."

A vote was immediately taken in Archer's presence and it unanimously elected him as executive director of Protestants and Other Americans United for Separation of Church and State.

Archer went home in torment. He did not honestly want to take on Americans United even though the idea intrigued and beckoned. When he went to consult with influential friends in Kansas, to a man they advised him to forget it. He was informed that the Supreme Court would soon be open to him and that this could be a stepping stone to the governor's chair. All his interests, predilections and affections lay in Kansas. Yet there was something about the invitation. . . .

On July 1, 1948 Glenn Archer wrote to Dr. J. M. Dawson: "As I view things I am personally ready to answer the call. If (the president and board) see the call as I do, I feel you may count upon my return."

What had happened to accomplish this complete turnabout? Archer says he had no intention whatever of going to Washington when he returned from the interview. Yet a few weeks later he wrote his acceptance. What happened would be inexplicable without the power of religion and will remain inexplicable to those who have never encountered it. One day Dr. Dawson called from Washington and said: "I just called to congratulate you for your acceptance of our position. You are to be our leader. The wife and I got the assurance of your coming at the family altar this morning, and I had to call you to tell you how happy we are that you will head this great cause."

Archer could only gape. It would not do to comment that God had failed to share the information with him. He could only stammer: "I'm pretty busy here." Dr. Dawson was not responsive to this. He hurried on: "Of course we have no office but you can work with me here in the Baptist building." He went on with the arrangements that could be made apparently with no doubt whatever that the matter of Archer's coming was settled. "The Lord will bless you. I'll help you. You have a great board and they will stand by you. Write me when you will arrive."

The assurance of Dr. Dawson shook Archer. But it was not this that decided him. Perhaps his motivation for acceptance can be put this way—that he accepted because he could not bear the burden of guilt that would have been his had he refused. It was the missionary call all over again. It was the Calvinist sense of the duty to do what God expected. One was not here merely to succeed at business; he was here to do God's Will. If this were God's Will—and it had all the painful earmarks of it—why then it had to be done. Response to religious calls was a family tradition. Glenn Archer's grandfather was a minister and so were the six sons of his grandfather Archer. Your grandparents could take it, he thought, but you can't. You with your nice house on the park. You with your comfortable career all set to schedule. What have you got in Washington? They haven't even mentioned salary! There will be none unless you raise it. All you have got is a cause. There's no money, no future in that. A man would have to be crazy to trade sure fire success for nothing.

Archer was in a trance. His tennis game folded. He taught corporation law by rote. He discussed the matter of a resignation with the president of the University. It would be accepted only if Archer insisted upon it. Two days later he wrote the resignation. He came to Washington, D.C. and started work in a garage behind the Baptist building with a borrowed desk and a borrowed typewriter. The total office supply investment was $10.54. Today Americans United is a flourishing enterprise owning its own headquarters building in the nation's capital. It has a readership of 200,000 for its handsome monthly review CHURCH AND STATE. It has three major regional offices in the east, middle west, and far west, and clearing house offices in a number of cities. It has chapters, committees, study groups in many centers. It is a known, feared and respected force in church-state issues. It has supported and both won and lost many significant church-state litigations.

Promotionally, Americans United has been a substantial success. It has purchased a desirable site in the nation's capital upon which to erect its new national headquarters building. Its members and supporting groups are in all the states and many foreign countries. Over a 20 year span no private organization of this nature has shown a comparable pattern of growth. It has enlarged its budget and staff and expanded its program in every one of these years and has made good on every single commitment. Americans United has gone forward in fair weather and foul without ever once looking back and is one of the most solidly established groups in America today. Except for the original note of $2500 (ninety day note) Americans United has never incurred a debt. It has been a cash basis movement without debts or deficits. It is the Archer way of business.

Americans United is not the lengthened shadow of this man. It is this man. He has identified himself with this movement and he has made it what it is.

The moment Archer agreed to become executive director of Americans United he began to reap the kind of calumny and abuse that were to be his lot the rest of the way. To backtrack a moment, I might observe that this kind of treatment for the organization itself had already begun. It began before Archer was on the scene or even thought of as director. The hostility of the Roman Catholic hierarchy was directed against Americans United from the moment of its birth. The Catholic leaders rightly sensed that their pressures for cultural domination and public subsidy had finally evoked an answering pressure. This new group if allowed to continue would surely be the stone in their road. It could conceivably block all their ambitions to draw tax funds for their support and to shape public policy to their purpose.

The Catholic leadership resorted to several devices in its attacks on Americans United. One was the pooh-pooh argument, that the thing would fall of its own weight within a year. Better weapons were the time-honored meataxes of personal villification and abuse. The first president of POAU was Dr. Edwin McNeill Poteat who was also president of Colgate-Rochester Divinity School in Rochester, N. Y. The Rochester diocesan bishop of the Catholic Church, James E. Kearney, immediately blasted Dr. Poteat as a communist, a religious bigot, an anti-Catholic agitator. Msgr. Hart, chairman of an Interfaith Goodwill Committee, charged that POAU was a divisive group seeking to make Rochester a "city of Interfaith Bad Will." The Catholic *Courier Journal* of the Rochester Diocese in its issue of January 15, 1948 carried this charge and also alleged that Dr. Poteat was attempting to turn Rochester into a "sort of national center for bigotry and religious hatred." The article then went on to charge as communists not only Dr. Poteat but also Dr. Mackay, Dr. Newton and Bishop Oxnam, perhaps the nation's best known Protestant leaders. Their crime was being founders of Americans

United, that stone in the Catholic path. Most of the continued harassment of these men because of their alleged "communism" can be directly attributed to this Catholic hostility over their association with POAU.

The Catholic objective so far as Dr. Poteat was concerned was quite clear. They were after his job. The idea was to create such a furor in the business community of Rochester that Dr. Poteat's position would become untenable. In this they were successful, or at least partially so. Dr. Poteat's problems mounted rapidly in Rochester and before long he resigned at the Divinity School to return to North Carolina as pastor of the Pullen Memorial Baptist Church in Raleigh.

Glenn Archer himself promptly began to feel the effects of Catholic hostility. A good example was the business boycott launched against him by a Roman Catholic priest in Logan, Kansas. Archer owned a lumber company in his home town of Densmore. The company had been supplying materials for the construction of Father J. T. Koegan's new church. On learning of Archer's acceptance of the post with Americans United, Father Koegan wrote to him on August 4, 1948:

I understand that you hold the major interest in the Home Lumber Co. of Densmore. From this firm we have been buying for our new church structure just about all of the material. . . . You have been profiting thru our building program—and now you would become part of a group which would tear that church and all it stands for down! I do not mind so much doing business with those who, through ignorance or otherwise, happen to be bigoted, but it is a different matter when it is a question of doing business with anyone whose livelihood is bigotry. The decision which we must make is being made unwillingly, but the decision is yours, not ours.

Father Koegan was not content with his own personal boycott of Archer's business. He talked and urged boycott among the Catholic community in the county. This lasted for seven years and nearly managed to tumble the business into bankruptcy. Archer relates an incident at the funeral of John Stenger, Jr. who had been killed in Korea and brought home to Kansas for burial. Since Archer had been a longtime friend of the family and happened to be visiting his old home, he attended the funeral which was conducted by Father Koegan. The priest used the funeral occasion to vent his hate upon Glenn Archer, denouncing him by name before all his tenants, relatives and friends as a "stooge of Joe Stalin" who was working against God and country. Feeling ran so strong against Archer that many of his old friends would not speak to him after this attack.

After the funeral of a local banker, Boise Wiltrout, Archer chanced to encounter Father Koegan. "How are you, Father?",

Archer asked, extending his hand. Said the priest: "You'll have to wash your filthy hand before I will shake it."

That was going too far. When this became known in the community, feeling turned against Father Koegan. He shortly found it advisable to ask for a transfer from the parish he had served for 24 years. When Archer spoke at Grand Island, Nebraska he was pleasantly surprised by a delegation from his old home who informed him after the meeting that Father Koegan had left the community, a victim of his own bitterness.

Archer soon discovered that Father Koegan's bitterness was symbolic. As the days and weeks passed he began to realize that he would often be confronted with the intransigent hatred of the leaders of the nation's largest church.

But for seven years Archer fought two battles—one in Kansas to save the family businesses; one in Washington to launch a new movement. He won both. As he puts it, "The Lord helped me both places. He gave me oil in Kansas and Joe Dawson's faith in Washington."

In its dealings with Americans United Catholic leaders had one objective—never to let the issue be faced on its merits. The issue was a simple one—should the United States arrangement of separation between church and state be changed to one of public sponsorship and subsidy of the church? The Catholic hierarchy was out to make the change; Americans United was opposed to it. That was the issue. Of course Americans United was opposed to any kind of religious establishment, whether Protestant, Catholic, Jewish, or general. The movement had a deep, ingrained suspicion of functional collaboration between state and church, however noble the purpose envisaged. Yet the practical effect of the *Manifesto* was to pit the organization directly against the United States hierarchy of the Roman Church. This group, and this group alone, was agitating consistently for a change in the church-state arrangement.

Catholic Action had as one of its top objectives the concealment of the real issue from the general public. This it did by various propaganda ruses. It claimed, for example, that government aid to Catholic schools was something altogether different from government aid to Catholic parishes and clergy. This despite the fact that the school and the parish were an integral unit under the same management and both owned by the diocesan bishop as "corporation sole." It argued that the government could provide aid for children in Catholic schools without aiding the schools themselves. It argued that since 90 per cent of the training in a Catholic school was in secular subjects the government could subsidize 90 per cent of the school without providing any aid to religion. Even the nomenclature the Catholics insisted on was rife with slick propaganda. Bills designed to provide transportation to parochial schools were called "fair bus bills" and the Catholic leadership insisted on this designation in the press. The whole controversy was called one over aid to "private" or "independent" schools even though more than 90 per cent of the schools involved were Catholic schools.

But by far the most effective device of all was the Catholic skill in raising the bogey of anti-Catholic persecution or of "bigotry" as it was called, whenever anyone dared to oppose the Catholic program. Although Roman Catholicism was the largest religious grouping in the United States, although Catholics were an absolute majority in three states and dominated the culture of most of the great cities of the country, Catholic leaders could readily take up the whine line and plead that they were being persecuted. They could do this and get away with it even at a time when their own power was becoming oppressive in many sectors. They could succeed in the gambit because scarcely a century ago Catholics had experienced a hard time in the United States and had suffered discrimination because of their faith. As it turned out this proved to have been a fortuitous development since Catholic leaders were able to exploit the memory even at a time when the shoe had quite passed to the other foot.

In 1956 Glenn Archer addressed the Southern Baptist Convention in Kansas City. Nineteen fifty-five and nineteen fifty-six had been years of aggressive and militant Catholic Action. In the New England states the Catholic leadership was using its vast membership as a power bloc to wring out public concessions for its parish schools. Bus transportation was already being sought in Maine and Connecticut. Through pressures on appropriate Congressional leaders Catholic Action had been passing one bill after another in "war damage claims" which were to result in the erection of a handsome Roman Catholic cathedral in Manila and the creation of a vast Catholic school system to rival the public schools in the Philippines. Cardinal McIntyre had announced his advocacy of a "G.I. Bill of Rights" plan to provide federal aid for Catholic schools. The Catholic censorship program was in full swing. Catholic pressure barred the great film "Martin Luther" from TV in Chicago and elsewhere. There were daily cries for an exchange of envoys between the United States and the Vatican. The Catholic Welfare Conference had already shown its ability to tie up aid-to-education legislation in Congress unless its schools received some of the funds.

In his speech at Kansas City, Archer addressed himself in specific terms to the Catholic power play. He charged that:

In the opening phase of this drive modest goals are sought. Then, as progress continues, the goals become more and more ambitious as deference becomes preference, preference becomes monopoly, monopoly becomes domination, and clerical domination spells the doom of personal salvation as evangelicals understand religion.

He continued, addressing himself to specific problems:

When the Roman Catholic Church demands an American ambassador to the Vatican this demand is not aimed at the spiritual regeneration of either America or the Vatican. . . . The aim is to secure public recognition of Roman Catholicism. . . . The end sought is prestige, advantage, power for this politico-religious organization.

That was plain talk. It was, of course, entirely true but it was the kind of truth which professional Protestant brotherhooders and Catholic Actionists were conspiring to keep from publication. Archer went on:

When the Roman Catholic Church seeks public subsidies for its activities in this country, this is part of the great, world-wide Vatican movement that drives toward cultural and political dominance everywhere.

This, too, was laying it right on the line. The gauntlet was taken up by Archbishop Edwin V. O'Hara, the Catholic prelate of Kansas City. Instead of meeting Archer on the issue, the Catholic bishop resorted to the "hurt reaction" and heaped personal slander upon his critic. He likened Archer to the Know Nothings and the Ku Klux Klan and invited the Kansas City chapter of the National Conference of Christians and Jews to join in the attack on Archer. In short, the archbishop resorted to the personal smear as the most effective way of handling the situation. Perhaps in this way he could keep Archer off major programs. He kept carefully to the practice of never facing the issue but rather throwing mud in the public eye.

On the urgent invitation of prominent Kansas City leaders, Archer promptly returned to defend himself. An overflow meeting was held on a hot Sunday afternoon at Second Presbyterian Church, August 26, 1956. A great crowd gathered to hear Archer's "Reply to the Archbishop." Bill Gremley, a Roman Catholic who served as director of the Commission on Human Relations, persuaded the police to detail two officers with conspicuous pistols in holsters to go to the church on the pretext that they were needed to "preserve order." Archer was described as an "out of town agitator" who might create a disturbance. The maneuver was part of the effort to categorize Archer as a low form of humanity to whom decent people would pay no heed.

The use of the National Conference of Christians and Jews in the endeavor to smear Archer was interesting. This was a favorite device of the Catholic leadership. Catholic leaders dreamed of the day when they could get the Conference to attack POAU as a "hate group." This, they felt, would be a most effective way of destroying the group's growing influence. On two occasions priest members of the national board of the Conference of Christians and Jews pressed their demand for an official denunciation of Americans United. Once the demand was shunted aside when John Sutherland Bonnell, minister of the Fifth Avenue Presbyterian Church of New York City, began to read some choice passages from a book, "Freedom of Worship" by Father Francis J. Connell of Catholic University. This was so much more rabid against Protestants than anything the priests could attribute to Americans United against Catholics that they subsided in confusion. At another time Dr. Albert P. Shirkey, Archer's pastor, pleaded with the National Conference of Christians and Jews "not to persecute one of my finest Christian members." Eventually the leaders of the National Conference of Christians and Jews proved to be too wary to be trapped. The hoped for denunciation of Americans United as a "hate group" never materialized.

All this makes clear the tortuous path Glenn Archer had to tread as the director of the new, struggling organization dedicated to preserving separation of church and state. He was greatly aided in his struggle by the continued willingness of the group's distinguished board members to lend their names to the enterprise. They were all busy men with heavy responsibilities of their own. They could not help Archer directly. But they did lend their names and their names were just impressive enough to blunt the Catholic effort to smother Americans United with a bigot blanket.

All of these men, with one exception, continued to serve on the board without flinching until their retirement and even beyond. They were an impressive lot: Dr. Charles Clayton Morrison, Dr. Edwin McNeill Poteat, Dr. John A. Mackay, Dr. Louie D. Newton, Dr. Joseph Martin Dawson, Dr. Charl Ormond Williams, Dr. Clyde W. Taylor, Dr. Frank H. Yost, Dr. W. Stanley Rycroft, Rear Admiral Harold C. Fitz, USN (ret.), Elmer E. Rogers, E. H. DeGroot, and many others. The only man to resign was Dr. Ellis H. Dana, executive of the Wisconsin Council of Churches who quit in 1964. Dr. Dana fell victim to the ecumenical movement. He began to feel that his presence on the board of Americans United was hurting him in ecumenical circles where any opposition to Catholic demands was being viewed as in bad taste. When Dr. Dana voiced a desire for change in Americans United he was promptly named chairman of a committee of the board to make a study and advance proposals. Dr. Dana's procedure was to invite two non-members of the board to perform these functions. This he did without consultation with his committee and before his committee had even met. When opposition to the chairman's course was heard from the committee Dr. Dana announced that all his efforts to change Americans United had failed and that he was therefore resigning. He then wrote a pamphlet attacking the organization and tried to sell it for 25c, inserting advertisements in various religious journals. As one of his colleagues on the board remarked: "That tree fell and the forest never missed it."

It was a rough road. Glenn Archer traveled it with complete assurance. This was what he had to do. He nurtured the new organization with the skill of a fencer, the dedication of an evangelist, and the determination of Martin Luther.

The blend of cause and man in Glenn Archer's leadership of Americans United is remarkably complete. He was, and is, an American unashamed. He really believes that the United States is a wonderful nation raised up by God for His purpose. Religiously he is Protestant and Methodist and is very proud of this. His Americanism—dare we use the word?—and his Protestantism are prominent facets of the man.

Separation of church and state became his life. To build an organization capable of bearing and supporting that concept became his life-long obsession. Some of his speeches reflect this fact. For it was an amazing characteristic of the man that he wrote his own speeches—always. I have written a score of speeches for him; others on the staff have written speeches for him. He never used any of them. To be sure he would pick up ideas here and there to work on, but the speech that emerged after long struggle and anguish was always his own. Usually he sat up most of the night before a big appearance hammering the thing into final shape. He would fret and fuss over it until he had it just the way he wanted. To an extent beyond that of any public figure of our time, with the possible exception of Adlai Stevenson, Glenn Archer's speeches are an authentic expression of the man.

A good idea of Glenn Archer's credo is contained in this passage from a speech "Out of Bounds" delivered in Constitution Hall, Washington, D.C., January 21, 1954.

I believe the government of the United States is based upon the finest principles of statecraft ever conceived by man, and that our country does indeed have a glorious tradition of freedom. If there is anything that is central in the concept of freedom, it is the unalterable insistence that the mind shall be free, that dissent shall not be punished by authority, that even the most "heretical" taxpayer shall not be taxed in order to propagate religious doctrines that are abhorrent to him or agreeable to him. True religion is never a product of compulsion or government sponsorship. Spiritual life is never the byproduct of church affiliation for political reasons.

Glenn Archer was indignant at the apparent use of the ecumenical movement by Catholic Action to blend Protestants into a bland consensus of support for Catholic political programs. The force of his indignation was directed at the Protestants who permitted themselves to be duped. One of his speeches called "Protestants Unashamed," delivered on a number of occasions in 1958, aimed at this problem. The speech stirred the animosity of the leaders of whom and to whom he spoke. But no one could miss his meaning:

The religious issue in American life today is posed by the drive of America's largest church for tax funds and other preferred status before the law. . . . The brotherhooders overlook this drive entirely. They consider it bad form to mention it. But they overlook, too, that if this issue continues to be ignored and its historical antecedents forgotten, it will erupt in an agony of bitterness such as our nation has never known. . . . The brotherhood boys are nice to have around but they may be more dangerous than the bigots.

This kind of leadership is sterile and bankrupt. We must publicly disavow the oft-repeated clichés of these men that they, and they alone, speak for Protestants. Those who betray Protestants are not entitled to speak for them. What these leaders deserve is not brotherly solicitude but resounding repudiation.

Glenn Archer's conviction shines through this peroration of an address, "The Growing Struggle for Religious Liberty," delivered in 1956:

Something is happening to the United States of America. A basic change in its culture is threatened. The land where religious liberty and justice have been guaranteed by the separation of church and state is now facing one breach after another in the historical wall of separation. . . .

We stand for something that is as native to America as the sand hills of Georgia, the wheat fields of Kansas, and the redwoods of California. . . . We are not only defending; we are affirming the principle which we believe to be integral to the America we love. That principle is this—that every man shall be free to profess and practice the faith he believes, and that the power of the state shall never be exercised in the service of religion.

One of Glenn Archer's most dramatic addresses was that before the Southern Baptist Convention in Dallas, Texas in June, 1965. The Elementary and Secondary Education Act of 1965 had just become law. Some Baptist leaders, caught up in the political "consensus," had chosen to wink at the church-state complications and to approve. Furthermore administrators of many Baptist colleges were being desperately tempted by the millions in federal funds which would be theirs if they would only nod their head. Archer did not seek refuge in vain rhetoric. He addressed himself directly to the problem the Baptists were then facing and he spoke with great candor. He told the Baptists bluntly that if they took public funds for their institutions these would, in time, become public. Using as his theme Esau's sale of his birthright, Archer said:

If Southern Baptists become an arm of the government, they stand to lose their people, their independence and their religion. Their churches will become liturgical and not saving, ritualistic and not redeeming. And when they discover their bad bargain, it may be too late.

He then added a eulogy to free churches in a free country:

In America religion flourishes more than any other place in the world. Here the Gospel is a mighty force. Here millions of dedicated churchmen and women sacrifice to support the work of their churches. Here men dig deep into their own pockets to build schools . . . without coercing others to foot the bill. And here a man's religion still means more than it does anywhere else in the world.

Approaching his 20th year as executive director of Americans United, Glenn Archer could survey with some satisfaction the edifice he and his colleagues had built. To the gratification of some, and the consternation of others, the movement has persisted and grown. Any serious appraisal of the church-state tradition in the United States today must take account of it.

One of the marks of Archer's wisdom was that he understood that Americans United was not a personal movement of his. The movement was always more than he was. It was there before him; it would be there after him. He was always thinking of the future. He began to plan for the transfer of his leadership to other hands. His ambition was not to take the movement to the grave but to have it thrive and bear its witness long after he was gone. Perhaps his most significant achievement lay in the erection of a structure so skillfully fashioned that it gave every evidence of permanence. It was a structure soundly built to stand storms and stress. An issue had brought Americans United into being. He wanted to build an organization that would persist as long as that issue itself.

Myron Taylor,
President Roosevelt's
personal representative
at the Vatican,
and
Pope Pius XII.

chapter **IV** **THE BIG ISSUES**

At least four major church-state issues have confronted Americans United during the years since its establishment in 1947. There has been a continuing spate of lesser problems as well. The four that reverberated across the nation were: (1) President Truman's appointment of General Mark W. Clark as U. S. Ambassador to the Vatican State; (2) the issue of the Roman Catholic Cardinals from the United States voting in the papal election of 1958; (3) the questions raised in connection with the candidacy of a person of Roman Catholic faith for the Presidency of the United States; and (4) the issue of federal aid to religious schools.

An Ambassador to the Vatican

In 1951 just as Congress was about to adjourn, President Truman announced the controversial Clark appointment. To Mr. Truman's complete astonishment the appointment was greeted with an angry uproar. Bishop G. Bromley Oxnam, vice president of Americans United, complained that this "has driven a wedge into our American life. . . ." In an address to 3,000 at a POAU-sponsored meeting in Chicago, Bishop Oxnam charged:

Casuistical camouflage cannot conceal the fact that when the U. S. Government sends an ambassador to the Vatican it is actually sending a representative to the Roman Catholic Church. The Pope derives his influence not from his status as sovereign of the Vatican State but from his status as the head of the Roman Catholic Church. . . .

An exchange of ambassadors between the United States and the Holy See was a longstanding ambition of the latter. Through its American arm, the National Catholic Welfare Conference, the Vatican had exerted steady pressure for such an appointment. The whole Vatican diplomatic corps which represented exchanges with 58 countries was an archaic survival of the days when the popes were political rulers of Italy or considerable portions of it. When the papal domain shrank to 108 acres the Vatican clung, nevertheless, to its far-flung chain of nuncios as its envoys were called. Countries like the United States with no formal exchange of envoys had Vatican representatives called Apostolic Delegates.

On the face of it, there would appear to be justification for raising the question as to why the Vatican needed all this. Why should it continue to play at international power politics when it no longer ruled a sovereign state worthy of the name? The expense involved was obviously terrific. Besides, hundreds of priests were diverted from parish work where they were sorely needed to social posturing in the diplomatic drawing room. German Bishop Joachim Ammann on October 16, 1963, electrified the Vatican Ecumenical Council during its 1963 session by teeing off on the entire corps. The whole diplomatic entourage was a waste of money and time, he said, and ought to be abolished. He charged that this apparatus put the church squarely into the business of international power politics which was no place for it to be.[1]

Bishop Ammann's arguments seemed to be sensible enough but they never appealed to the professionals at the Vatican who loved the tinsel and regalia of the diplomatic brigade. Besides, the Vatican always insisted as a condition of a diplomatic exchange that its man should be dean of the diplomatic corps with top ranking at all social and ceremonial functions. Here was real prestige and the Vatican firmly clung to it.

President Roosevelt had appointed Myron C. Taylor as his "personal representative" to the Vatican in 1939. Taylor's staff was paid for by the State Department funds though the whole appointment was of dubious legality. President Truman discontinued the personal representative operation but eventually appointed Mark W. Clark as full ambassador to the Vatican. The Clark appointment was worse than a blunder; it was a mistake. The amazing thing was that Mr. Truman, one of the shrewdest politicians ever to live in the White House, should have made it. On this point, as is the case with many professional politicians, he simply did not understand the temper of the country.

Glenn L. Archer did understand. He sensed here an opportunity to reach the nation with the POAU message on separation of church and state. It was about this time that Archer first met Paul Blanshard, author of *American Freedom and Catholic Power*. Paul Blanshard was a unique composite of preacher, politician, social worker and saint. He always reminded me of the old Oxford Group "absolutes." He had all of them but above all he had that absolute honesty. He was, and is, one of the very few completely honest men I ever met. He carried objectivity about himself and his own effort to what I thought were unnecessary lengths. He was meticulous and punctilious about everything he did. He was altogether incorruptible in both public and personal life. He was desperately feared by Catholic leaders because, of all the critics with whom they had to deal, he was one who could be counted on to tell the truth, the whole truth and nothing but the truth. This can be a terrifying thing.

Paul Blanshard had published his *American Freedom and Catholic Power* with the high hope that it might sell 10,000. He was most fortunate to draw violent Catholic "bigot" attacks against the volume with carefully organized efforts to suppress it. This is the best kind of promotion a book can get. The sales eventually topped 300,000 and made Blanshard financially secure for life. The book first published in 1949 had already made Blanshard a celebrity. When he and Archer met in the summer of 1951 shortly after the Clark appointment, it occurred to the latter that a series of great public meetings of protest would be a successful operation. Blanshard was engaged for a series of addresses at protest meetings. He would receive $25 and expenses for each lecture.

The meetings sponsored by Americans United featuring Paul Blanshard as speaker were a smash hit from coast to coast. They drew some of the greatest crowds since William Jennings Bryan and Billy Sunday. Blanshard appeared in 40 cities. Other speakers brought the number of meetings to more than 120. The effort spanned the nation. Three thousand turned out in Los Angeles, 3,000 in Chicago, 6,000 in St. Louis, 3,500 in Cleveland, 3,000 in Cincinnati, 3,000 in Nashville with many turned away. The average was well over 1,500 at all the meetings. Success of the endeavor was also due to the sound promotional work of John Chapman Mayne, a St. Louis Council of Churches official, who had joined the staff of Americans United as Director of Organization. Mayne knew how to promote a public meeting. He would do the advance work, take up the collection, lay the groundwork for a future organization in the city, then dash on to the next place. Many of the subsequent chapters and study groups of Americans United had their inception in the great Blanshard meetings.

What were the motivations behind the appointment of a Vatican ambassador? The main motivation was, of course, political. It was just the kind of maneuver that would appeal to any politician: it would butter up the Catholics without doing any particular harm. Catholics could be counted on to be flattered at this official recognition of the ruler of their church and would be inclined to vote for the responsible man or party at the next election.

The State Department has consistently urged the diplomatic exchange with the Vatican. This is due to the fact that the Department is always interested in building up its own apparatus. The more diplomats the bigger the department and the greater the appropriation. This is an occupational disease which afflicts all divisions of government. The argument offered by State officials is that the Vatican offers a good "listening post." This means that the Catholic Church with its clergy in many countries of the world has a kind of pipe line from them to its central organization in Rome. An ambassador at the Vatican would be able to pick up, via gossip or otherwise, reports that would be helpful to the United States.

The principal arguments adduced by opponents of the exchange are that the appointment would really be that of an ambassador to the Pope as a religious figure, thus giving official preferential treatment to a church; that the Vatican is itself such a politico-religious blend that official recognition of the political is impossible without official recognition of the religious as well; that such an appointment would violate the United States' longstanding policy of separation of church and state; that the proposal would be creedally divisive.

In an address to 3,500 at a rally sponsored by POAU in Constitution Hall, Washington, D.C., January 15, 1953, the Rev. Leland F. Stark, then rector of Epiphany Church of that city and now the Episcopal Bishop of Newark, N. J., decisively finished off the arguments for an exchange of envoys with the Vatican. Dealing with the "listening post" contention, Bishop Stark questioned "the morality of a great nation like our own seeking to use a church for espionage value." He pointed out that the United States already had an ambassador in Rome, one accredited to the Italian Government. An ambassador to the Vatican would also have to office in Rome, he contended, because there would be no room for him at the Vatican proper. He then went on:

Would it be so complex . . . a problem for an authorized Vatican official to put himself in touch with our ambassador in Rome? Must we wreck the Constitutional policy of church-state separation, which has served us well since our very birth as a nation, just in order that the Vatican can call one American diplomat on the second floor of the American Embassy in Rome instead of one on the first floor?

The bishop-to-be closed with a ringing affirmation:

We Protestants together with millions of other Americans are as strongly united as ever against any interlocking of the official processes of our government with the official processes of any church, such as involved in a Vatican envoy, be he a personal representative of the President or a full-fledged ambassador.

Washington was not long in hearing from the grassroots. The White House and members of Congress as well began to get communications from constituents on the Vatican ambassador issue. The eventual result was the largest tide of mail ever to reach Washington on a single issue, before or since. One senator said that he had personally received more than 60,000 letters protesting the Clark appointment. For this Americans United was preeminently responsible.

Cardinal Spellman assumed a "hurt" stance. He just could not understand it. He said that as an American citizen he favored the appointment. He expressed "surprise" that senators of high principle and intelligence should be opposed. He was particularly distressed at the Jewish opposition since Catholics had not objected to United States recognition of Israel! But the avalanche had started and nothing could stop it. President Truman was licked and he knew it. Mark Clark asked that his name be withdrawn. The President announced that no new appointment was contemplated at that time. That was the end of that—until the next time.

Challenge to the Cardinals

The next public issue which drew nationwide attention to Americans United for Separation of Church and State was the organization's protest over the Catholic Cardinals from the United States voting in the papal election of 1958 which resulted in the naming of Pope John XXIII. The POAU protest cannot be understood apart from the issue described above—appointment of a United States Ambassador to the Vatican. At the time the State Department was pressing for the appointment, Americans United had engaged in an extended controversy with the Department over this issue. The Department had insisted the State of Vatican City was a political entity, however miniscule its territory, and that it was perfectly proper to name an envoy to the political entity without in any sense involving matters of religion.

The Department had a technical argument. The 108 acre tract was there. It had a *de facto* existence. It was in a sense a political state ruled by the Pope as its dictator.

In the fall of 1958 a beautiful opportunity occurred to smoke out the State Department on this issue. It was an opportunity that offered grave risks as we soon discovered, but it was just too good to pass up. Eight U. S. Code 1481 of the Immigration and Nationality Act provided that any U.S. citizen be deprived of his nationality for "voting in a political election in a foreign state." Many Americans who unwittingly cast such ballots had, in fact, been deprived of their citizenship. Very well: why not take the State Department at its word! If, as its officials had argued for so long, the Vatican State was a political entity to which an envoy could duly be sent, then certainly the election of the head of that state would be an election in a foreign state and no American citizen could cast a ballot without losing his nationality! Specifically affected were Cardinal Francis Spellman of New York and Cardinal James Francis McIntyre of Los Angeles. Certainly these men ought to be warned before they voted at St. Peter's.

I shall never forget when I proposed this idea (which originally came from a member on the West Coast) to Paul Blanshard who by then had become special counsel for POAU. He roared with laughter but soon turned serious and thought for a long time. "There are grave risks in it," he said. "There will be repercussions among the Protestants who will not understand what we are trying to show. But it is so good that I would recommend we risk it."

Paul Blanshard had the best brain I have ever encountered. Nor was his power that of naked intellectualism. He coupled with it an astute sense of public relations. He could tell you in advance with startling accuracy what public reaction would be to a given proposal. He hit this one squarely. The protest was a nine day wonder and attracted thousands of new subscribers, but we did get into trouble.

Eventually we decided that the best way to approach the matter would be by letter to Secretary of State John Foster Dulles. Just a short time before, in 1957, Glenn Archer had written to the State Department to inquire about the legality of the receipt of papal political awards by Congressmen John W. McCormack and John J. Rooney when this would appear to be barred by the Constitution. In his reply Loftus E. Becker, legal adviser of the Department, stated that "The United States . . . recognized the fact that the Vatican City is a sovereign state." Congress itself apparently recognized this fact when it passed a special law extending permission to Representatives McCormack and Rooney to receive these awards of a foreign state. The POAU letter to Secretary Dulles began with this fact and also cited a statement of Cardinal Spellman himself that "The Holy Father is not alone the Supreme Head of the Catholic Church. He is also the head of a sovereign state."

The letter then documented with legal citations, 10 cases in which Americans had been deprived of their citizenship for voting in a foreign election. It pointed out that "this is the first papal election under the Immigration and Nationality Act, or its predecessor laws which have contained this provision . . ." Then the letter concluded:

Our government should be consistent in matters of church and state law, and it should insist on a policy of church-state separation. Our courts have declared that religious preference in the administration of our laws is illegal, and this rule should apply to the mighty as well as to the humble.

The State Department did the only thing it could do. It immediately shifted ground, began to play down the political aspects of Vatican City as a state and to magnify the role of the Pope as the head of a church. The Department's Loftus E. Becker included no legal or legislative citations in his reply to Mr. Archer. He could do no more than write:

In the Department's view the real significance of the election of a pope is religious—the fact that the individual elected becomes the Bishop of Rome and titular head of the Catholic Church—and it is only incidental and by virtue of his office as head of the Catholic Church the Pope is also head of the State of Vatican City. Accordingly, the Department is of the view that the papal election is not a "political election."

In a form letter sent to many who inquired about the strange situation, Raymond T. Yingling, assistant legal adviser, developed the thesis. In a manner reminiscent of the "Two Powers" theory in Catholic thought, Mr. Yingling suggested that the Pope "is both head of the Roman Catholic Church and, in a distinct and separate capacity, Chief of State of the Vatican City." Then, apparently sensing the weakness of his contention, he also resorted to the argument that the Pope was "only incidentally" head of the State of Vatican City.

The best one could say for this was that it constituted a poor performance. Probably it was the best the Department could do under the circumstances. Its officers must have regretted their previous unequivocal pronouncements about the Vatican as a political entity since their problem was now to mute the political and accentuate the religious. Americans United had made its point, however. Its leaders had a new arsenal for the next battle over an ambassador to the Vatican. They were now armed with strong statements from the State Department that the Pope was primarily a religious figure. When the Department would begin new agitation for an ambassador to the Vatican Americans United would ask why such an appointment was contemplated when the State Department itself had acknowledged that the real significance of the Pope lay in the fact that he was a religious leader and that he was but incidentally a political ruler. Then the inevitable question: Why should the United States send an ambassador to a religious leader? This move cut the ground from under the Irish Catholic politicians in Congress intent on having a hearing on the Vatican and earmarking funds for sending a Vatican delegate at some future date.

This strategic gambit was pretty well lost on a portion of the public, however. The issue was a bit too subtle for general consumption and it was not generally consumed. Our mails were heavy with letters from angry Catholics who seemed to feel that we had impugned the honor of Cardinals Spellman and McIntrye. In equal number were the protests of sentimental Protestants who accused us of launching a "home to Rome" movement for the two prelates. Even members of the board felt the fury. The only criticism on strategy I ever had from Bishop G. Bromley Oxnam, vice president of Americans United, was occasioned by this episode. He listened to my explanation of what we had hoped to achieve by the voting challenge, then replied that he thought it was, nevertheless, "misunderstood." He pointed out that there was still a mood of mourning for the late Pope which made the injection of such an issue not in the best taste. Also, that the entire religious community thought of the election of a Pope as a purely religious matter and simply would not comprehend what we were getting at.

I should point out that Bishop Oxnam commended us on many occasions for what he considered to be good achievements. This was, I repeat, the only question he ever voiced to me. I am still inclined to feel that on balance the move was wise. Millions of people did get at least a slight introduction to the church-state dilemmas which persistently impale the Vatican. While State Department officials by occupation are an elusive breed we did get them about as near a corner as they will ever come. That in itself was something. At least two State officials got a chuckle out of our move and admitted "it was real smart."

In a letter addressed to *The New York Times,* December 10, 1958, I wrote:

In our challenge to the citizenship of the Cardinals we did want to point up our contention that the Vatican is a split personality, posing first as a state, then as a church, claiming the advantages of both yet refusing to accept the consistent role of either. Such ambivalence may be profitable to the Vatican, but we believe it to be inimical to the interests of a nation which has separated church and state. This ambivalence should be exposed and resolved so far as American civil policy is concerned.

[1] Concilio Ecumenico Vaticano II, Ufficio Stampa, Session No. 2 News Bulletin No. 13, General Congregation No. 49, October 16, 1963.

Glenn L. Archer defends his organization against a charge of "bigotry" at a meeting of the National Conference of Christians and Jews in Washington, D.C., 1963.

Dean Francis B. Sayre, Sen. Eugene J. McCarthy, Lawrence Spivak, moderator, Glenn L. Archer and Dr. John A. Mackay. "The Big Issue" was telecast June 1, 1958.

V THE RELIGIOUS ISSUE IN THE 1960 ELECTION

chapter

The 1960 election campaign brought Americans United its days of greatest strain. At the same time this episode brought an unprecedented opportunity to educate the American public in regard to church-state separation. POAU had always opposed certain Roman Catholic policies on church and state but it had always insisted that no Catholic should be barred from public office merely because of his personal faith. The organization had never specifically supported or opposed any candidate for public office. What should be its attitude during the difficult period of the Nixon-Kennedy campaign, when, for the first time, a Roman Catholic seemed to be within striking distance of the White House?

The prospect of a Catholic candidate on one of the major tickets fired up religious antagonisms. There were those who hated the idea of a Catholic—any Catholic at all—either on the ticket or in the White House. Such persons wanted to use Americans United as a weapon to defeat such a candidate. We could not lend ourselves to any such operation. There were those who wanted to use the campaign that eventually involved a Roman Catholic candidate, John F. Kennedy, as the occasion for an anti-Catholic crusade. This sort of thing had to be rigorously opposed.

Many consultations were held in Washington concerning this important policy question. Special counsel Paul Blanshard was at this time in Vermont working on a book concerning Spain and Portugal. In 1959 he had produced a work, *God and Man in Washington,* in which he had stated the problems that might be posed by the presence of a Catholic in the White House and also warmly praising the then Senator John F. Kennedy for his frank statements in behalf of the separation of church and state. He praised him so warmly, in fact, that Sen. Kennedy had sent him a word of personal thanks for the fairness of his analysis.

Paul Blanshard prepared for the board of Americans United a proposed policy statement for the campaign. After careful study and appraisal it was accepted with very few modifications. The statement was published in CHURCH & STATE, also in *The New York Times* and many other newspapers.

Unhappily, the POAU policy statement was published on the same day as a statement by a new group formed under the leadership of Dr. Norman Vincent Peale. The juxtaposition of the two statements in the public press was most unfortunate since Americans United had no connection with the Peale committee. The public was confused by the fact that the statements of the two groups appeared on the same page and tended to lump both together. Professional enemies of Americans United cultivated the confusion and promoted it for their own ends. The Peale committee was so bitterly attacked in the press that Dr. Peale soon withdrew from it.

This incident called attention to the extremely difficult role of Americans United. There was a grave danger, which such an episode strengthened, that the entire church-state issue involving the candidacy of a Roman Catholic would be swept under the rug with the spurious plea of "intolerance" or "bigotry." We at Americans United headquarters were determined that this must not happen. Thus we were caught between the brotherhooders on the one hand, and the fanatics on the other. It was hard to say which were worse!

The statement authored by Paul Blanshard set a fair and proper course to which we meticulously adhered throughout the campaign. The statement warned against any display of religious prejudice in connection with the 1960 conventions and election. However, it pointed out with candor that Catholic candidates for President should be "scrutinized with particular care." The reason?—

Because their church has taken a definite stand against the Supreme Court's interpretation of separation of church and state, and particularly against the denial of public money to sectarian schools. Their church leaders have also expressed opinions favorable to the appointment of an American ambassador to the Vatican. To challenge every Catholic candidate on these issues is a wise and necessary precaution designed to protect our American traditions.

Then came the crucial part of the statement—"Questions for a Catholic candidate." These questions were to become famous during the 1960 election campaign. Originally, there were four; the fourth called attention to the oft-reiterated stand of the Roman Catholic Church in regard to birth control and asked whether the candidate would be bound by this position in regard to foreign aid and domestic policy. Some members of the board objected and this question was dropped. In retrospect it appears that it might have been wise to include it. The other questions were:

1. The Canon Law of your church (Canon 1374) directs all American Catholic parents to boycott our public schools unless they receive special permission from their bishops. Do you personally approve or disapprove of this boycott rule?

2. The bishops of your church in an official statement in November 1948 have denounced the Supreme Court's interpretation of the religion clause of the First Amendment and have urged that the Constitution actually permits the distribution of public money on an equitable basis to sectarian schools and other sectarian institutions . . . What is your personal attitude toward your bishops' interpretation of the Constitution, and toward the new plan for financing parochial schools?

3. Many nations recognize your church as both a church and a state and send official ambassadors to the Holy See. If you become President what would be your policy concerning the appointment of an American ambassador or a personal representative to the Vatican?

Every conceivable effort was made by Catholic apologists to "bigot" their way out of the troublesome predicament in which the questions placed them. The Catholic press cried "bigot," "foul," "religious prejudice," "Ku Klux Klan" and strove eagerly to raise all the old goblins. Catholic leaders and political leaders as well sought the aid of a group called the Fair Campaign Practices Committee. This group had been organized to call attention to unfair tactics being used by any candidate or party.

In March, 1960 a meeting was held in New York City under the auspices of the Fair Campaign Practices Committee with the idea of discussing the problem of unfair use of religion in the election campaign. No one from the staff of Americans United was invited, which appears odd in view of the fact that Americans United was a principal object of discussion. It soon became evident that a Catholic priest, Msgr. Francis J. Lally, editor of the *Boston Pilot,* hoped to secure from the committee some kind of public denunciation of Americans United. The *Boston Pilot* is one of the most reactionary of the Catholic diocesan publications, second only to the *Brooklyn Tablet.* But it is the Boston diocesan publication—the diocese of the Kennedys. It was rumored that Msgr. Lally had refused to attend the session if any member of the Americans United staff were invited. Whether or not this was the fact, the inclusion of Msgr. Lally and the exclusion of our staff were both accomplished. Msgr. Lally took a great deal of the committee's time attacking Americans United. He saw that a denunciation of the group by the Fair Campaign Practices Committee would not only promote the Kennedy candidacy via a "fair and free of prejudice" appeal but would also strike a heavy blow at Msgr. Lally's number one enemy, Americans United.

The Fair Campaign Practices did not take the bait, however. Eventually it took the position that while it was not proper to judge any candidate on the basis of his religion, it was proper, nevertheless, to question a candidate about the bearing of his religious faith on issues relevant to the office he seeks. This was precisely the Americans United position.

Chief spokesman among Catholics in the attempted hush-hush of the religious issue was the late Gustave Weigel, S.J. Father Weigel sought to bury the matter once and for all in a widely quoted interview with the press.[1] Fr. Weigel's strategy was to equate Roman Catholic clerical directives with "conscience" and plead for its inviolability. He failed to mention a single one of the specific questions that Americans United had raised. He insisted that the realms of political concern and religion were separate and distinct. Never did he address himself to the problem which occurs when a "moral directive" of an absolutist church conflicts with an official's civil duty.

A good example of the smear and dodge tactic was offered by Father John A. O'Brien of the Notre Dame University faculty and a long time consultant for the National Conference of Christians and Jews. In a story prepared for *Look* magazine, February 16, 1960, Father O'Brien was asked this question by the interviewer: "How do you explain the fear of some Americans that the separation between church and state will break down if a Catholic is elected President?" He replied:

> *I believe this fear is chiefly the result of the 12-year propaganda campaign by an organization called Protestants and Other Americans United for Separation of Church and State, which follows the same line of attack on Catholics the Know-Nothings followed in the 1850's. The campaign has been intensified because a Catholic may be candidate for President this year. Of course, the current attacks have no more basis in fact than those of a century ago.*

Fr. O'Brien's charge against Americans United was of course entirely false. It was a bit of McCarthyism with a double design—to damage the principal antagonist of Catholic demands on the state and to obscure the real "religious issue" which a Catholic candidate for President posed.

Catholic leaders and politicians alike persisted in their endeavor to confuse the public by claiming that anyone who mentioned the matter of Catholic stands on certain public policies was making attacks on that church. This went regularly on despite the fact that Americans United had specifically declared that there could be no possible question about a Catholic's eligibility for the presidency and that such a matter could not properly be raised. Cardinal McIntyre made a violent attack on the organization's position. He was quoted in the *New York Times*, January 16, 1960 and again on June 24, 1960 and in many other papers as saying that it was "very un-American" to raise the issue of religion in regard to a man's qualification for the presidency. He even asserted that a candidate should not be questioned in regard to his views on church-state relations because that was "a question for the Legislature and the Judiciary."

Even after the campaign was over the Catholic leadership held to its view that to raise any issue whatever in connection with a Catholic's candidacy was a dirty business. Atlanta Bishop Francis E. Hyland wrote to his diocese:

We have passed through a rather bitter presidential campaign, during which our holy faith was assailed unjustly from many quarters. In some cases the attacks proceeded from ignorance; in other cases it would be difficult to avoid the conclusion that malice was the motivating force.

There were also Protestants who wanted everyone to vote the Democratic ticket to prove how big and tolerant he was. Joining the attack on Americans United were the liberal extremists of Union Theological Seminary, New York City—Dr. Reinhold Niebuhr and Dr. John C. Bennett. The two theologians attacked the position of Americans United urging that the group did not "represent Protestants." The statement sought to convince the country that Niebuhr and Bennett really did represent Protestants. In a carefully worded editorial November, 1960, CHURCH AND STATE pointed out that Niebuhr and Bennett were not the impartial and disinterested Protestant spokesmen they represented themselves to be. They were, said CHURCH AND STATE, "professional politicians since both were vice presidents of a political party committed to one political slate." CHURCH AND STATE also pointed out that Niebuhr and Bennett were both unreliable on the church-state issue, that both had attacked the Supreme Court's doctrine on church-state separation in 1948, and that both had favored use of public funds in aid to church schools.

There had, to be sure, been some use of the presidential situation as an occasion for attacks on the Roman Catholic

Church. This had been minimal, however, in comparison with the tide of determined, scholarly concern to raise the legitimate question of what a President who was a member of an authoritarian church might do when confronted with policies of that church which were opposed to those of the nation he led. Out in the middle west the *Catholic Messenger* of Davenport, Iowa, May 12, 1960, did make a grudging effort to acknowledge some ground for legitimate concern. But the spirit of its utterance largely obviated its effect. After a highly prejudicial account of the situation, Msgr. J. D. Conway wrote:

In some of these notions prejudices are freely mixed—prejudices fomented by Paul Blanshard and POAU—and though these tend to anger us, we should not immediately rule all these questions merely offensive and out of place. Some of them are asked honestly and they should be answered with patience, if the questioner is willing to listen.

Though the Catholic leadership might endeavor to cover the "religious issue" with a bigot blanket the candidate himself, John F. Kennedy, quickly realized that this would be impossible. One might have done it in a race for mayor or even governor, but here the thing was too sensitive and there was too much at stake. There was some evidence that Senator Kennedy did originally feel the whole issue could be handled by crying "bigot." Thousands of members of Americans United sent the "Kennedy questions" directly to the candidate by mail and telegraph. He originally replied to them with a form letter which attempted to divert the whole matter into a "religious test" for public office. He wrote:

Aside from being somewhat insulting to the many legislators and other public officials who have served their country faithfully and in accord with the Constitution, I think that the mere presentation of a list of questions such as you have suggested betrays a dangerous tendency which is not consistent with the spirit of our Constitutional principles. I refer specifically, of course, to the Sixth Amendment (he meant the Sixth Article of the Constitution) *which forbids the promulgation of a religious test for holding public office.*

This was a good try. In a lesser campaign it might have succeeded, but for the presidency it was no go. When a man like Arthur Krock of *The New York Times* insisted that Senator Kennedy would have to face the religious issue candidly he began to see the light. He realized that if he wanted to be nominated and elected the thorny religious issue must be met head-on. Once he had made this decision Kennedy moved straight ahead and never looked back. He met the religious issue as forthrightly as his most skeptical critic could have demanded. He virtually put his critics in the position of having to accept his assurances on the subject as satisfactory and therefore as removing the religious issue from consideration. Their only alternative was to say that Kennedy was a liar and not to be trusted on anything—a position that responsible leaders could not assume. His candor on the religious issue won the 1960 election for John F. Kennedy.

Perhaps the clearest and most complete presentation of the religious issue to the nation occurred during the NBC Meet the Press TV program June 1, 1958. Appearing on the program monitored by Lawrence Spivak were Glenn L. Archer, executive director of Americans United, and John A. Mackay, the organization's vice president. The format also included Dean Francis B. Sayre of the Washington Cathedral and Senator Eugene J. McCarthy of Minnesota. Addressing 40 million viewers Archer once more put the now famous questions that had been posed in CHURCH AND STATE. He elaborated carefully on each one and explained its relevance. He concluded his presentation with this careful phrasing:

I believe it is time and perhaps proper to ask and to answer two questions: When is it time in this country for a man to use the high office of the Presidency for the advantage of his church? My answer is, Never. When may a man of any faith be elected to the Presidency of the United States without discriminating against any church? My answer is, Any time.

Dr. Mackay put his finger carefully on the religious issue. He said:

The concern is grounded on the particular nature, the unique character of the Roman Catholic Church. In three respects, this great religious communion is unique. First, the Roman Catholic Church is a state as well as a church. . . . Two, the Roman Catholic Church makes for itself unique claims. It claims to be superior to the state. . . . Third, . . . when the situation is favorable . . . then the ideal is expressed as in the Spanish concordat, that the state in Spain must recognize that the Roman Catholic faith is the sole religion of the Spanish nation.

Dr. Mackay concluded his presentation with the observation "that in the last quarter of a century there has appeared in American life what has been characteristic of Latin countries for centuries, namely, the tremendous reality of clericalism."

A study of CHURCH AND STATE and other items published by Americans United prior to and during the election campaign demonstrates that the line so carefully chosen was as carefully pursued. In retrospect we can say that we achieved everything that we could have hoped. The religious issue was not swept under the rug. It was faced and discussed in as open and proper a manner as could have been expected in the emotional throes of a political campaign. It is true that there was some religious prejudice exhibited during the campaign both by those who voted for a man because he was a Catholic and those who voted against a man because he was a Catholic. Some things were spoken and written that should have been omitted. This has been true of every election campaign, however. In an overall judgment we are entitled to say that the American people can be proud of the way the delicate and highly inflammable religious issue was handled in the 1960 election campaign.

The real significance of the Americans United contribution to the campaign can only be discerned in the fact that John F. Kennedy did eventually face the religious issue and deal with it. What apparently precipitated the Kennedy church-state credo was a letter from Glenn L. Archer, executive director of Americans United, which went to Senator Kennedy late in December of 1959. This letter pointed out that in the view of millions the senator had been evasive and unsatisfactory in his position on the religious issue. Archer called on Senator Kennedy to proclaim his American "credo" as Al Smith had done in 1928. The letter bluntly warned the senator that he was ill-advised in the way he had handled the religious issue to that point. The text of the Archer letter follows:

Dear Senator Kennedy:

I personally have a great deal of admiration for you and I agree with you on many important national issues.

I thought you were ill-advised to say what you did about our questions. We have no desire to infringe upon a man's religious beliefs, but when a church takes one position and the tradition and law of the nation is another, it seems important to us to find out how important national characters feel about some of these matters.

I am sending you a copy of our CHURCH AND STATE Review. I have tried to be very fair in presenting this material. I'd like to know your reaction. . . . What you say and think is not only important to our 80,000 leaders scattered over the nation, but is important to the nation and to the world.

Sincerely,

Glenn L. Archer
Executive Director

There is no doubt that this letter was a considerable factor in the abrupt shift in the candidate's handling of the religious issue.

On three occasions Senator Kennedy addressed himself directly to this issue. The first was in an interview for Look magazine with Fletcher Knebel, recorded in its issue of March 3, 1959. At least two of the POAU questions were answered incisively. In regard to the question of federal aid to religious schools, the Senator said: "I'm opposed to the Federal Government's extending support to sustain any church or its schools."

On the issue of an ambassador to the Vatican, he said: "I am flatly opposed to the appointment of an ambassador to the Vatican. Whatever advantages it might have in Rome—and I'm not convinced of these—they would be more than offset by the divisive effect here."

In an address before the American Society of Newspaper Editors in Washington, D.C., April 21, 1960, Senator Kennedy asserted that he was opposed to federal aid to parochial schools since this was "clearly unconstitutional." He also paid his respects to the issue of possible clerical control over his official performance. He said:

There is only one legitimate question underlying all the rest: Would you as President of the United States, be responsive in any way to ecclesiastical pressures or obligations of any kind that might in any fashion influence or interfere with your conduct of that office in the national interests? I have answered that question many times. My answer was and is No.

The only one of the POAU questions which Senator Kennedy had not directly met was the one relating to the Canon Law that barred Catholics from sending their children to the public schools unless the bishop was willing to make an exception. In his meeting with the Protestant ministers in Houston, Texas, September 12, 1960, Senator Kennedy declared himself "against unconstitutional aid to parochial schools and against any boycott of the public schools (which I have attended myself) . . . ."

Senator Kennedy won the election at Houston. He climaxed his appearance before the Protestant ministers by declaring that if ecclesiastical pressures should mount to the point where he could no longer resist them, could no longer perform his duties without regard to them, he would resign as President, "and I hope any conscientious public servant would do the same." The ministers believed him; the nation believed him. CHURCH AND STATE described the Houston speech as a "ringing declaration of steadfastness in resistance to clerical pressures," and quoted with approval the statement of Dr. Henry Pitt Van Dusen that Senator Kennedy had given "a clear, and unambiguous affirmation of his stand on the controverted issues contrary to his Church's position."[2]

Political and clerical buncombe did, of course, persist throughout the campaign. Americans United patiently persisted in its effort to keep the religious issue in its proper perspective. In its October, 1960 issue, CHURCH AND STATE editorialized:

Nothing in the presidential campaign so far has disgusted us so much as the tendency of newspaper editors and columnists

to oversimplify the church-state issue by describing it in terms
of personal prejudice . . . We also prayerfully hope that personal
religious belief will not play a part in this campaign. But when
an editor assumes that American apprehensions about a Roman
Catholic President . . . are confined to "religious belief" alone,
he is evading the real issue. It must be remembered that a
Catholic President will belong to an organization that, everywhere in the world where it has the power, demands a partial
union of church and state, with political treaties or concordats
designed to protect its privileges, with political ambassadors,
with public appropriations for church schools and sometimes
for the salaries of priests, and with official Vatican-supported
suppression of Protestantism in such countries as Spain and
Colombia.

The same editorial praised Senator Kennedy for "disowning
some of the policies of his own church."

In a concluding editorial November, 1960, "The Tumult and
the Shouting," CHURCH AND STATE recognized that the
fundamental controversy in which it was involved would go on
regardless of how the election came out. The journal said:

If Vice President Nixon wins, the bishops will continue their
drive for tax support both in the Congress and in the states. If
Senator Kennedy wins, the bishops will do the same thing. The
campaign to change the American tradition in church and state
will go on.

POAU proposes to continue its legal and educational program regardless of who wins and who loses. We shall defend the
money line against the predatory assaults of any church—even
the largest and strongest. We intend to do this before as after
and after as before.

One additional matter should be mentioned in connection
with the organization's role in the 1960 election campaign. This
related to the so-called Knights of Columbus oath. Copies of the
alleged Knights of Columbus oath had been in circulation for
close to 50 years but during the 1960 election campaign they
were printed and circulated in large quantities. The oath purports to be the obligation assumed by Knights of Columbus
when they are initiated into one of the degrees of that organization. It states in bizarre language what all the fledgling knight
promises to do to opponents of other faiths and what all should
be done to him if he fails. How this fantastic "oath" originated
it is difficult to say. Some say that the Knights did originally
have such a commitment, that it was changed about 1912.
Others say that the oath is actually a counterpart of one taken
by members of the Jesuit order at the present day. This charge
has some verisimilitude since the Jesuit order was born in the
brutal days of the Counter-Reformation and probably has never
changed its commitments.

Whether the "oath" had originally some factual basis or was simply composed out of whole cloth by a crazed mind, it certainly was not the oath being taken by Knights of Columbus in the 1950's. Americans United investigated the matter thoroughly, found that the oath of the Knights was a rather innocuous commitment that had nothing in common with the blood and fury thing that was being attributed to them. In 1958 and 1959 inquiries about the Knights of Columbus "oath" showed a sharp increase at POAU headquarters. We were getting as many as a dozen a day and there were indications that the thing was being circulated widely.

Circulators of the "oath" lent a coloration of authenticity to the project by declaring that the item had been inserted in the *Congressional Record* of February 15, 1913. This was a fact. The alleged "oath" had been printed in the Chester (Pennsylvania) *Republican* during a Congressional election of 1912. One of the candidates, a Mr. Bonniwell, who was a member of the Knights of Columbus, attributed his defeat to this incident. A Congressional Committee investigated the matter and strongly condemned the printing of such "false and libelous" material. The text of the spurious oath was inserted in the *Record* as an example of bigotry and to accentuate the committee's condemnation of the tactic.

Americans United was sending out a form letter containing this information about the spurious "oath." As the inquiries increased the staff concluded that it would be wise and helpful to release the results of its investigation to the nation. This was done in a carefully prepared release February 9, 1959. The release declared that "after careful research we are convinced that the 'oath' is fraudulent and should not be circulated by anyone." The statement further observed: "It seems strange that credence should be given to a manifest fabrication of this sort, yet we are convinced that the 'oath' is being more widely circulated than ever and that it is gaining acceptance in new quarters."

After a complete rehearsal of the facts regarding the appearance of the "oath" in the *Congressional Record* the POAU statement then advised that misguided persons who had circulated the "oath" as authentic had been prosecuted and punished by the courts. The statement added:

Since the false "oath" has been circulated in connection with political campaigns, we feel that a warning should be issued well in advance of the 1960 election campaign. It is particularly appropriate in view of the possibility of a Presidential candidate of the Roman Catholic faith.

Since Americans United had frequently been associated in the mind of the public with criticism of the Roman Catholic Church, the appearance of such a statement, which was widely circulated in the press, practically killed off the Knights of Columbus "oath." Circulation of the item shrank to a trickle and little was heard of it during the campaign. In a further helpful gesture Americans United sent copies of the "oath" and its analysis of it to the Fair Campaign Practices Committee.

[1] *New York Times*, September 28, 1960.
[2] November, 1960.

John F. Kennedy
on the campaign trail.

chapter VI JOHN F. KENNEDY AND FEDERAL AID TO RELIGIOUS SCHOOLS

Americans United was involved in so many exciting church-state
issues that it is difficult to choose appropriate ones to describe
here. There was the famous expose of church "unrelated business" operating under the blanket of church tax exemption which
Americans United was the first to make. This involved the
famous controversy with the Christian Brothers in which we
defended the position that church distillers should pay the same
tax as their secular competitors. The basic problem of the "unrelated business" of churches remains unsolved, however, and
must likely await legislative relief.

Americans United pointed up the growing seriousness of the
problems posed by tax exemption for church property with its
study, "Tax-Exempt Religious Property in Key American Cities"
—the first study of its kind. We were concerned with the church-
state involvements in urban renewal programs and supported a
number of famous lawsuits seeking to adjudicate such issues.
Also with the transfer, free of charge or at nominal cost, of valuable government properties to churches under the Surplus
Property Disposal Act. Clerical obstruction to public birth control programs in domestic and foreign aid legislation was an
early and constant preoccupation. We have also raised the issue
in connection with sectarian hospitals which receive public
funds while operating under a sectarian medical code which
bars birth control information and equipment.

Efforts to exploit space trips for sectarian promotion, to
attach official sectarian symbols to various divisions of the
armed forces, to manipulate "shrine sites" for sectarian advan-

tage, to associate sectarian symbols with official places and programs, and to produce sectarian postage stamps and coins, have all been opposed by Americans United. Abuses of the government free mailing privilege on behalf of sectarian groups, donation by local governments of real estate to churches, church gambling operations in defiance of local laws, sectarian infiltration into the Peace Corps and sectarian manipulation of the Agency for International Development, the problem of civil judges and other officials who put sectarian commitments above their civil duty, provision of free public services to churches by municipalities, controversies in 22 states over publicly provided transportation to religious schools and free textbooks for these institutions, the problems of religious exercises and teaching in the public schools, investigation of religious bias in government hiring, investigation of religious freedom problems in Spain, Latin America and in connection with the Vatican Ecumenical Council—these are a few of the issues with which we have worked. The list could be made 10 times as long.

There is no difficulty, however, in picking the fourth of the "big issues" for detailed presentation. This one wins hands down.

The fourth big issue with which Americans United has been continually involved, and likely the biggest of all, is that of government aid to religious schools. We have already seen in Chapter I how this was the immediate issue which triggered Americans United into existence. We also indicated there the propaganda gambits by which the Roman Catholic leadership would seek public aid for its denominational schools.

There were several facets of the problem. Basic, perhaps, was the decision of the Roman Catholic bishops of the United States not to patronize the nation's public schools. As compulsory education laws developed, and as the determination not to place Catholic children in the public schools hardened, the necessity for a system of Catholic parish schools was manifest. The Baltimore Plenary Council of 1884 finalized school arrangements on the basis of instructions received directly from the Vatican:

Near each church, where it does not yet exist, a parochial school is to be erected within two years from the promulgation of this Council, and is to be maintained in perpetuum . . . [1]

Then, when the separate school structure was erected and was educating some five million at the elementary and secondary levels, the Catholic leadership discovered that its members were unwilling to pay the bill. The leadership was thus confronted with the necessity of cutting back, or rather, not expanding the system, or of finding other sources of revenue. The Catholic leaders sought tax support as they had done many times in other nations and, indeed, as they had previously done in the United States in the 1840's.

The decision to boycott the public schools was made first on the basis of Canon Law 1374. The text of Canon 1374 reads:

Catholic children may not attend non-Catholic, neutral, or mixed schools, that is, those which are open also to non-Catholics, and it pertains exclusively to the Ordinary (Bishop) of the place to decide, in accordance with instructions of the Holy See, under what circumstances and with what precautions against the danger of perversion, attendance at such schools may be tolerated.[2]

The boycott was also inspired by Catholic minority psychology. The public schools which emerged on the American scene in the middle decades of the nineteenth century had at least a faint coloration of Protestant faith. The religious practices which persisted in these institutions were Protestant in character as the overwhelming majority of the population was of that faith. Also, the academies which had been the predecessors of the high schools had been predominantly Protestant. There was not only the exclusiveness imposed by Canon Law but also the problems of ethnic and religious minorities struggling to preserve their faith in the face of cultural pressures.

During the nineteenth and twentieth centuries, therefore, the American strategy of the Catholic hierarchy was two-fold: to use the courts to eliminate all religious teaching from the public schools under the establishment clause of the First Amendment, and to give just as many Catholic children as possible a controlled Catholic education in separate, denominational schools. Their reasoning on the first point is to be seen in the statement of Archbishop John Hughes of New York who pleaded in 1848:

Let not the Protestant version of the Scriptures, Protestant prayers, Protestant hymns, be forced upon the children of Catholics, Jews and others, as at present, in the schools for the support of which their parents pay taxes as well as Presbyterians.[3]

Catholic parents with the encouragement of their bishops fought out the issue of public school Bible reading and prayer in the courts of the land. The famous *Engel* and *Schempp-Murray* cases of the 1960's represented the final success of this phase of the Catholic program. By this time Catholic plaintiffs had been replaced with Jewish, Unitarian and atheist plaintiffs, but the objective sought was exactly the same—protection of children under compulsory attendance laws from religious indoctrination in the schools. By this time, however, some of the

Catholic bishops felt sufficiently assured in their cultural pre-
dominance to indulge themselves with the luxury of attacking
the Supreme Court for its "godlessness" in giving them precisely
the decision they had sought for a century. Francis Cardinal
Spellman of New York said he was "shocked and frightened"
by the decision. "The decision strikes at the very heart of the
Godly tradition in which America's children have so long been
raised."[4] Richard Cardinal Cushing of Boston said: "To me
it is a great tragedy that the greatest book ever published and
a constant best seller cannot be read in the public school
system of education." Archbishop Patrick A. O'Boyle of Washington, D. C. said the ruling clears the way for the deletion of
all expressions of religion in the country's public life. Archbishop Robert E. Lucey of San Antonio, Texas: "Now that
God has been banished from our public schools, I fear that the
Declaration of Independence is in jeopardy. . . . It is one of the
most magnificent state papers in our history, but it teaches
religion, and if God must go, the same fate awaits the Declaration."[5]

The Catholic determination to withdraw its children from
public schools and educate them in a separate system encountered rougher going. It was, in fact, never more than half successful. Catholic laymen had serious misgivings about the
program and, from the first, objected to clerical exactions for
schools when they were already paying for a perfectly good
system which their priests forbade them to use. In the 1860's
there was a strong movement among Cincinnati Catholics to
merge the competitive systems into one mutually satisfactory
system. The Catholic Archbishop John Purcell at first appeared
to give the movement some encouragement. But when the final
negotiations were underway he dashed the hope of merger by
a blunt communication in which he said:

> *The entire government of public schools in which Catholic
> youth are educated cannot be given over to the civil power. We
> as Catholics cannot approve of that system of education for
> youth which is apart from instruction in the Catholic faith and
> the teaching of the Church. If the School Board can offer any-
> thing in conformity with these principles as has been done in
> England, France, Canada, Prussia and other countries where
> the rights of conscience in the matter of education have been
> fully recognized, I am prepared to give it respectful considera-
> tion.*[6]

There were numerous controversies at the local level over
the dual school systems. Local authorities have sought by one
means and another to end the expensive dualism and to iron
the two systems together. The many lawsuits supported by

Americans United over "captive schools" were really concerned with this issue.[7] All the talk of "shared time" or "dual enrollment" represents merely another of the many efforts to solve the local problems created by the existence of a separate, denominational system of considerable dimensions.

Having established their denominational school system and having labored to build it up, the Catholic bishops eventually found themselves with an immense, costly structure which they could neither be rid of nor yet adequately maintain. Of course they did not want to be rid of it. They wanted to include within its walls all Catholic children in the United States. This was always impossible and as time passed it became even more so. The fecundity of Catholic families was so great that their children simply could not be accommodated in Catholic schools. The enforcement of Canon Law against parents who insisted on patronizing the public schools became largely academic. As at least half the Catholic children could not be admitted to Catholic schools, it was easy to evade the rule. The situation had, moreover begun to worsen in the late forties. A trend commenced then which is proceeding at an accelerated pace today. Catholic citizens are becoming increasingly reluctant to pay both parochial school tuition and public school taxes. Inflation has caused school costs to skyrocket. The religious vocation has little appeal for modern Catholic women and the supply of teaching nuns has begun to decline. Even when new schools can be built there are no nun teachers for them. Lay teachers must be hired thus compounding the cost. The proportion of Catholic children educated in Catholic schools began a steady decline. In the sixties various dioceses undertook a program which had been long contemplated and long postponed: they began to cut back existing classes and to curtail enrollment.

The public system had been encountering many of the same problems. School budgets which used to pass in a breeze now encountered heavy going. For the first time in the history of the public schools bond referenda began to be voted down. Many educational leaders began to voice the view that the only solution lay in federal aid to education. They argued that the real estate tax, long the base for school support, was no longer adequate. For one thing, the proportionate share of tax-exempt property had rapidly risen and approached 50 per cent of the total in some cities. As local taxes mounted, more and more landowners sought exemption by one device or another. Taxes had mounted to the point where taxpayer resistance had become serious. Freeholders were apt to vote down anything they got a chance to vote on.

By contrast, the federal income tax appeared easy to tap for education. Here was money the taxpayers never had in the first place! Due to these and other considerations the drive for federal aid to education gained headway during the 1940's and swept to triumph in the late fifties and sixties. The Catholic estimate of federal aid was soon made and it was probably accurate: If public schools get federal aid and we do not, we are finished. The competition at which they were already losing would become a rout. This meant one thing—not the abandonment of the intolerable weight of the competitive system, as Mary Perkins Ryan, a Catholic woman was to suggest in 1963, but a renewed drive for public subsidy.[8] The hierarchy whose leader was Cardinal Francis Spellman, unofficial primate of his church in the United States, brought all its political pressures to bear upon one point—to block all federal aid to education programs until Catholic schools were included.

This was the strategy from the moment that federal aid was proposed. It was generally successful. No federal aid to education bill was passed that did not contain some benefits for religious schools, with the possible exception of the so-called "impacted areas" bill which aided schools in districts where unusual federal activity had imposed a strain upon the schools. Other than that, Cardinal Spellman and his colleagues held the line. The Defense Education Act of 1958 contained benefits for religious schools. The Higher Education Facilities Act of 1963 contained construction aid for denominational colleges. The student loan program included religious schools. So it went.

After the big try in 1957 there was a final effort in 1961 and 1962 to put through Congress a federal aid bill for public schools only. This effort failed. Since then there has been no attempt to pass such a bill. A number of aid bills have been proposed and passed since then, but all contain forms of aid for religious schools. The 1961-62 failure is of interest because it involved a bitter political battle between the first Catholic President, John F. Kennedy, and his own church. In this struggle Americans United was deeply involved.

The estrangement over the school aid issue between President Kennedy and the leadership of his church had its origin in the election campaign of 1960. I have already recorded how the then Senator Kennedy with his sure political sense realized that he must oppose the official Catholic line on this issue. He stood strongly against aid to parochial schools on the basis of the constitutional issue but was so decisive in his statements that he appeared to doubt its social wisdom as well. Then began a strange but beautiful friendship between President-to-be John

F. Kennedy and Americans United. There was, perhaps, a bit of embarrassment on both sides. There is no need to conceal that the inner circle of the organization was delighted with the Kennedy stand. It was the POAU stand, pure and simple! Not in many years had a candidate for the presidency expressed himself so specifically for separation of church and state. Senator Kennedy was not only for separation, he spelled out what it meant in money-line terms. For him it meant no federal aid for religious schools. This was exactly what it meant for Americans United—and for the Supreme Court. The painful editorial task in *Church and State* was to keep the reporting of Senator Kennedy's church-state stand in terms that did not seem to indicate our endorsement of his candidacy. We were, of course, barred by our charter from any political activity and had to be very circumspect. It was an exceedingly difficult period for us all—made so by Senator Kennedy's outspoken endorsement of our own church-state position!

It was difficult for him, too. He had no trouble with the Catholic voters. They had an earthy sense of the political realities and freely forgave the senator for his church-state credo. Many of them actually shared it; the rest understood the logistics of the campaign which had made such pronouncements necessary. But the Catholic leadership neither forgave nor forgot. As might have been expected Senator Kennedy's credo of independence from his church in political decisions drew the priests' wrath. The *Monitor*, official voice of the Trenton, N.J. Catholic diocese editorialized that Senator Kennedy had played into the hands of "crusading bigots."[9] The paper charged that by his statements the senator had "supinely accepted the imputation of disloyalty implicit in attacks of the church's chronic critics."

The Jesuit publication *America* described Senator Kennedy's handling of the religious issue as "appeasement of bigots," and insisted that he was wrong in discussing views about his religion at all.[10] It said that the questions asked him involving religion were "discriminatory, insulting and without pertinency . . ." The senator's espousal of strict separation was too much for Father Virgil C. Blum, S.J., mentor of the predominantly Catholic Citizens for Educational Freedom, a group set up to agitate for public subsidy to parochial schools. He complained:

It seems somewhat strange to see a Boston Catholic in the "strict separation" camp usually occupied almost exclusively by Protestants and Other Americans United for Separation of Church and State and its adherents . . . [11]

Father Blum then went on to bewail the fact that Senator Kennedy had apparently ruled out some of his (Blum's) pet schemes for channeling federal funds to parochial schools. He said:

Does he (Kennedy) mean to exclude tax credits or grants made directly to parents as violating separation of church and state? Does he mean to exclude the possibility of the Federal Government giving grants to denominational institutions to perform a specific educational task?

The *Providence Visitor,* official publication of the Catholic diocese of Providence, R.I., argued that Senator Kennedy had "overstated his case."[12] The editorial stated that the senator "seems to have pleased the POAU more than Catholic opinion." The *Visitor* said that Senator Kennedy would have showed real courage if he had refused to deal with the POAU questions at all and had declined to take a religious test "to allay suspicions of Catholic baiters." The *Indiana Catholic and Standard* took Senator Kennedy to task, saying that "when a man starts making a distinction between religion in 'private life' and as and 'office holder' he seems to be thinking like a secularist who wants religion totally separated from life."[13]

The self-styled liberal *Commonweal* and the conservative *Ave Maria* both blasted Senator Kennedy for meeting the religious issue. *Commonweal* insisted, contrary to obvious fact, that there was no official Catholic position on such a matter as aid to parochial schools. *Ave Maria* was critical because he expressed agreement with Supreme Court decisions barring use of public funds for parochial schools. It hinted that perhaps he had joined the ranks of those who wanted parents to be "unfairly penalized for exercising freedom of religion" in sending their children to religious schools.[14] A partial survey of the Catholic press indicates that in addition to those mentioned the *Catholic Free Press,* the *Denver Register,* the *Monitor,* the *Michigan Catholic,* the *St. Louis Review,* the *North Carolina Catholic* and the *Kansas City-St. Joseph, Mo. Register,* all attacked Senator Kennedy for the proclamation of his credo. Chief points of irritation were that he would not put ecclesiastical directives ahead of his civil duty and that he was opposed to public grants for parochial schools because the Supreme Court has ruled them unconstitutional.

Perhaps Senator Kennedy was almost nettled enough to change churches when he got the following from the St. Bernard Parish publication in Pittsburgh. The pastor, Father Joseph I. Lonergan, wrote:

If Senator Kennedy said what he is quoted as saying he does not know what he is talking about. Senator Kennedy does

*not have the background of Catholic philosophy and history
to discuss Catholic subjects. Therefore he ought to keep his
mouth shut on Catholic matters. All he can do is mislead
Catholics who do not know any more than himself.*[15]

As I have remarked, Catholic voters understood and forgave.
Ninety per cent of them marked their ballots for John F. Kennedy for President. But church officialdom remained harsh and
adamant. It was the Catholic lobby that defeated President Kennedy's general aid to education bill because it did not include
Catholic denominational schools.

What developed was a fantastic struggle between the first
Catholic ever to make the White House and the officialdom of
his own church. "The Bishops vs. Kennedy" was the title of
Fletcher Knebel's article in an apt description of the situation.[16]
Knebel quoted C. Stanley Lowell, associate director of Amer-
icans United, as saying: "We are extremely well pleased with
President Kennedy," and Paul Blanshard, its special counsel:
"If Kennedy sticks to his guns, he'll be re-elected with ease—
by Protestant voters."

Cardinal Spellman was so anxious to head President Kennedy off that he could not wait for him to get his chair warmed
and his program before Congress. On January 17, 1961 the unofficial United States primate, declared that it would be "unthink-
able" that any American child be denied federal aid to education funds because his parents had selected for him a "God-
centered (i.e. Catholic) education."[17] Even Msgr. Frederick G.
Hochwalt, Catholic educational lobbyist in Congress, urged the
Cardinal to wait until Kennedy had actually presented his
program and then had something specific to work on. The
Cardinal went ahead anyway. President Kennedy was shaken
but not daunted. In a message to Congress on February 20,
1961 he issued a call for federal aid to the nation's schools but
specifically excluded religious schools from his bill. He noted
that aid to such institutions was "clearly unconstitutional."
At a press conference on March 1, 1961, regarding aid to parochial schools he said: "There isn't any room for debate on
that subject. It is prohibited by the Constitution and the
Supreme Court has made that very clear. Therefore, there would
be no possibility of our recommending it."[18]

A hurry up meeting of key Catholic bishops and the nation's
Catholic Cardinals was held in Washington, March 2, 1961.
There was a long discussion. Some of the bishops were appre-
hensive of the clash with the nation's first Catholic President.
But when the vote came all present supported the Spellman
line. Catholic action would seek to defeat all legislation which

"discriminated" against Catholic schools. Speaking for all the bishops, Archbishop Karl J. Alter said:

In the event that a federal aid program is enacted which excludes children in private (parochial) schools, these children will be the victims of discriminatory legislation. There will be no alternative but to oppose such discrimination.[19]

The entire weight of Catholic political action was thrown in against President Kennedy in an effort to head off federal aid to public schools. The effort was entirely successful. Aid to public schools was killed in the 87th Congress by the Catholic lobby when the Kennedy Administration refused to meet its demands.

The death blow was administered by the House Rules Committee where the enlargement of that group was supposed to have provided a "liberal" majority. One of the new members was Rep. James J. Delaney who insisted on incorporating into the bill a provision for construction loans for parochial schools. When the Rules Committee favored keeping the two matters separate, Rep. Delaney, a close friend of Cardinal Spellman, cast his vote in opposition to school aid. This gave the opposition an eight to seven majority and killed the legislation in the 87th Congress.

Principal instrument in defeating Catholic demands in the 87th Congress was a legal memorandum prepared by attorneys in the Department of Health, Education and Welfare and the Justice Department. Americans United played a key role in the preparation of this memorandum which actually piloted the Kennedy Administration on the church-state aspects of the school aid question. The memorandum was transmitted to the Senate Subcommittee on Education, chaired by Senator Wayne Morse, by Abraham Ribicoff, then Secretary of Health, Education and Welfare, on March 28, 1961. There is colossal irony in the fact that this strict separationist memo should have come from Ribicoff, a man who has consistently used his influence in public life to break down separation of church and state.

The significant document entitled "Memorandum on Impact of the First Amendment to the Constitution upon Federal Aid to Education" recalls that the Supreme Court has held that:

The State has a legitimate concern with the health, safety and, indeed, education (of children). It may extend assistance in various ways to achieve these ends. But where this assistance is also assistance to a religious institution, the means become crucial. One horn of the Constitutional dilemma is that the State may aid a child to achieve a sound body and a sound mind; the other is that the State may not aid the religious instruction of the child.

> *To accept without qualification the theory that whatever benefits the child is ipso facto constitutional is to ignore the obverse prohibition. It either proves too much or proves nothing at all. The crucial question then becomes separating the permissible from the prohibited, the educational function from the religious one.*[20]

In endeavoring to indicate just what forms of federal aid would be constitutional and what forms would not, the memorandum flatly states that "Federal grants to sectarian schools for general educational purposes would run squarely into the prohibitions of the First Amendment as interpreted in the *Everson, McCollum* and *Zorach* cases."[21] (It might be noted in passing that to this list should now be added the more recent church-state decisions of the Supreme Court in *Engel v. Vitale, Schempp v. Abington* and *Murray v. Curlett* all of which follow the same line). The memorandum states:

> *Aid by way of grants to sectarian schools could only be justified by a reversal of the Supreme Court's interpretation of the establishment clause and a new interpretation which would regard it as merely prohibiting discrimination among religions. Whatever its historical justification, this latter interpretation of the clause has been urged upon the Court in the cases cited and rejected by nine Justices in Everson and by eight in McCollum. . . .*[22]

As to the argument based on "fairness," the memorandum points out that students attending religious schools do so as a matter of free choice. "If the choice is not 'free' it is because of the religious beliefs of the individuals making the choice, not because of governmental edict. Since the public schools are open to all children without exception, it cannot be argued that constitutionally prescribed discrimination exists."[23] Even long-term, low interest loans to sectarian elementary and secondary schools are also termed unconstitutional in the memorandum released by the government's attorneys. The memorandum holds that "The Supreme Court put transportation at the outer limits of the constitutionally permissible."[24]

It is an amazing fact (though hardly surprising!) that when hearings began on aid to education in the Johnson Administration, this pivotal document of the Kennedy Administration was scarcely mentioned and the only copious quotes from it were supplied by the representative of Americans United. The new Administration wanted a new doctrine of the First Amendment and it was forthcoming.

Before going into the new predicament confronted by Americans United with the election of President Lyndon B. Johnson in 1964, it might be helpful to give specifics on the objections to government aid to religious schools. The objection was, of course, constitutional in the first instance. We firmly believe that the First and Fourteenth Amendments as construed by the Supreme Court do bar public assistance to religious schools. We believe, further, that these constitutional strictures are based on wise social policy, that even if there were no law on the subject at all, it would be undesirable to use tax funds in this manner.

The distinction between aid to Catholic schools and aid to the Catholic Church itself is one that eludes us. As we see it they are one and the same thing. The integral relationship of Catholic schools to the total operation of that church is well stated by Justice Jackson in his dissent in *Everson v. Board of Education:*

> *I should be very surprised if any Catholic would deny that the parochial school is a vital, if not the most vital, part of the Roman Catholic Church. If put to the choice, that venerable institution, I should expect, would forego its whole service for mature persons before it would give up education of the young, and it would be a wise choice. Its growth and cohesion, discipline and loyalty, spring from its schools. Catholic education is the rock on which the whole structure rests, and to render tax aid to its Church school is indistinguishable to me from rendering the same aid to the Church itself.*[25]

The facts are irrefutable. The same ecclesiastical official who owns the church owns the school. Both are held in the diocesan bishop as "corporation sole." This official is appointed by the Pope and can be reassigned by him at any time. There are not two operations—a school and a church. There is a single parish operation. There are not two treasuries but one. The same priest who serves as pastor of the church also heads the parish school. The two institutions are characteristically housed in the same compound, directed by the same persons with programs carefully integrated each to the other. We do not have to do with two institutions—a church and a school. We have to do with one institution—a church.

In the conduct of the Catholic school the ecclesiastical officials in charge are not content with giving courses here and there in "religion." Their objective, as enunciated by Pope Pius XI is to permeate the entire curriculum with Catholic religion. This is true of mathematics and the natural sciences no less than of the social sciences. To speak of supplying public aid for the "secular courses" in a parochial school may be useful as a propaganda technique, but it has no substance in fact. There are no such courses in Catholic schools according to the oft-repeated statements of Catholic educators themselves. To support such a program with public funds is simply to support the church itself with public funds.

Catholic propagandists for public funds have apparently given up on the argument that most of the teaching in their schools was secular and could therefore be supported by public funds without violating the Constitution. Now they seem prepared to acknowledge that all their teaching is permeated with their particular doctrines but that it should be supported by public grants anyway. Said Father Blum: "Religious permeation does not change the secular nature or character of secular subjects."[26]

Auxiliary Bishop Clarence E. Elwell of the Cleveland, Ohio Archdiocese remarked that: "permeation by religion" ought to have "the same privilege granted permeation by secularism or any other 'ism' as long as the nonreligious subject matter is adequately mastered."[27]

But there is an even more fundamental issue—the control of education itself. In a democratic nation like the United States education has been free and compulsory. To insure the reality of such education it has seemed wise to provide a system of community schools, owned and operated by the public, thus providing an educational opportunity for every child. Under our system these are not government schools, not state schools. The schools belong to the people who own them, operate them, control them through duly chosen officials and pay for them by their taxes. The Catholic cry for "freedom of choice" in education is really a cry for clerical preemption of education. Shorn of its propaganda, the Catholic theory of education is that it ought to be run by priests. The American method of public education run by the people themselves is viewed as basically wrong and immoral.

In a pluralistic religious situation like the United States the Catholic appeal for tax support would, if successful, lead us toward sectarian fragmentation of education. The Catholic clergy would, in effect, be hired by the state to run schools for Catholic children. Other churches with sufficient numbers involved would likewise be hired by the state to educate their children. Those with smaller numbers could combine for school purposes or continue to patronize the remnants of the public system. The change which Catholic leaders are, in effect, advocating is from public to private (religious) control of education. All the pleas about putting God back into education, putting religion into the schools, etc. cannot obscure that fact.

The plain truth is that in a religiously pluralistic country like our own, this kind of education will be far less efficient than the public system. It will be far more expensive since two, or perhaps 202 systems, cannot be operated as economically as one system. The founders of Americans United clearly perceived this situation. In the *Manifesto* they called it to the attention of

> ... *the great body of educators throughout the nation, regardless of their religious affiliations, whose noble profession will be stultified by further encroachments upon the public school system or by the complacent acceptance of those already in force. The teaching profession perceives, perhaps more clearly than others, the evil social consequences in the permanent fissioning of American culture which will result from state support of church-controlled education.*

The defense of the Supreme Court's "tight doctrine" of the First Amendment became the first business of Americans United. Ours was to be an effort in education and litigation. The work of Americans United in litigation is described in another chapter. Our educational endeavors have always brought charges of "lobbying." As an educational, tax-exempt corporation we are forbidden by law to spend any substantial portion of our income in attempting to influence legislation. "Substantial" was described in several court cases as in excess of five per cent. It was generally understood that appearing at Congressional hearings as expert witnesses on legislation did not come under the ban. This was particularly true when we were invited to appear as was usually the case. Nor did our expression of editorial opinion in *Church and State* constitute attempts to influence legislation.

Anything beyond this kind of activity, at least on any large scale, was impossible for us. The situation was all the more maddening because the National Catholic Welfare Conference just a few blocks down the street engaged with complete abandon in all the kinds of legislative activity from which we were rigorously barred. Their representatives operated like professional lobbyists. They were in and out of the Congressmen's offices actually assisting in the drafting of legislation, putting a word in here and a word in there, cajoling, promising, threatening. We were under almost constant threat and investigation by the Internal Revenue Service. The Catholics never had an investigation or even the threat of one. They did as much lobbying as they chose and engaged continuously and massively in endeavors to draft and pass legislation and they did it all with perfect impunity. They had around them the protective armor of the nation's powerful church which no government official in his right mind would think of challenging. There is not the remotest justice in this situation, but these are the facts of life in the United States today.

The Catholics were constantly complaining about us to Internal Revenue and that service was always quick to follow up the complaints. If we pointed to Catholic lobbying or National Council of Churches lobbying all we got was a hearty laugh. I recall a small town politician in Wickliffe, Ohio named Robert P. Woodman who made attacks on Americans United a kind of political platform. He was always writing letters to Internal Revenue complaining about our "lobbying activity" and urging that we be deprived of our tax exemption. He would send copies around to as many newspapers as he could and some would publish them. Once he even got William F. Buckley of the *National Review* to take up his cause and urge Internal Revenue action against Americans United.[28] Neither Woodman nor Buckley ever got around to mentioning the legislative activity of their own church which was a Niagara compared with our dribble.

If they were taxed with the patent injustice of this, Woodman and Buckley would probably have replied that since the Catholic Church had such vast wealth and such a tremendous annual income, it could, in fact, spend many millions on influencing legislation and still come within the five per cent restriction mentioned in the regulations. Americans United, on the other hand, with a modest income could spend very little for this purpose. That is about the way the present law arranges it: a wealthy church can do all the lobbying it wishes but a poor organization like Americans United can do none.

All this had direct bearing on the church-state situation for, in the fifties and sixties the matter became largely one of legislative concern. The Catholic Welfare Conference's educational division headed by Msgr. Frederick G. Hochwalt, was exerting tremendous political pressure to obtain federal aid to parochial schools. There was really no formal opposition especially after much of the old line Protestant leadership capitulated and began to help the Catholics get what they wanted.

[1] *Church, State and Freedom*, Leo Pfeffer, Beacon Press, Boston (1953) page 427.

[2] T. Lincoln Bouscaren and Adam C. Ellis, *Canon Law, a Text and Commentary*, Third Revised Edition, 1957, Bruce Publishing Co., Milwaukee, page 744.

[3] Leo Pfeffer, op. cit., pages 295-296.

[4] *Columbia Journalism Review*, Fall 1962, page 5.

[5] *The Dialogue*, "The Supreme Court, Bible Reading and Prayer," July 1963 National Conference of Christians and Jews, Bulletin No. 24.

[6] Leo Pfeffer, op. cit., page 379.

[7] See Chapter VII.

[8] Mary Perkins Ryan, *Are Parochial Schools the Answer?* Holt, Rinehart and Winston, New York, 1963.

[9] *Monitor*, February 27, 1959.

[10] *America*, March 7, 1959.

[11] *Brooklyn Tablet*, February 28, 1959.

[12] *Providence Visitor*, February 27, 1959.

[13] *Indiana Catholic and Standard*, February 27, 1959.

[14] March 2, 1959.

[15] A parishioner sent us a copy.

[16] *Look*, May 23, 1961.

[17] *New York Times*, January 18, 1961.

[18] *New York Times*, March 16, 1961.

[19] *Washington Post*, March 3, 1961.

[20] "Memorandum on the Impact of the First Amendment to the Constitution upon Federal Aid to Education, Dept. of Health, Education and Welfare, March 28, 1961.

[21] Ibid.

[22] Ibid.

[23] Ibid.

[24] Ibid.

[25] 330 U. S. 1, 24.

[26] Virgil C. Blum, *Freedom in Education, Federal Aid for All Children*, Doubleday (1965) New York, page 86.

[27] *New York Times*, April 23, 1965.

[28] *National Review*, August 10, 1965, pages 681-682.

Dr. Gerald E. Knoff, Department of Education, National Council of Churches, Paul Blanshard, special counsel Americans United, and Methodist Bishop Charles Wesley Lord at a hearing of the House Subcommittee on Education in Marcy, 1961.

VII chapter THE JOHNSON CONSENSUS: FEDERAL AID TO RELIGIOUS SCHOOLS

The assassination of President Kennedy in November, 1963 brought Lyndon B. Johnson to the Presidency. He subsequently won election in his own right in 1964. His election campaign and election created an altogether new church-state predicament. Whereas President Kennedy had to please the separationists and to prove his purity on all such issues by taking the hard line, President Johnson was under no such compulsion. John F. Kennedy had the Catholic vote in his pocket. It made little difference to Catholic voters that he had pledged that no federal funds would be expended for parochial schools. He was their boy, the first with a real chance for the top spot, and that was enough.

President Johnson had quite another problem. True, he had sources of strength that President Kennedy did not have. But he also had to woo the very vote that President Kennedy never had to think about at all. He could and did let the word go around that he, a Protestant, could do more for the Catholics than the Catholic Kennedy. He not only could, he would. A way would somehow be found to give the Catholic leaders what they were demanding. Some kind of formula would be devised to skirt the constitutional issue in federal aid to religious schools.

This was practical politics. It was what President Johnson felt he must do to win. He did get the Catholic vote. Not quite the way President Kennedy got it, but enough to put him over. Needless to say, the advent of his administration created an entirely new church-state climate in the nation and multiplied the problems of Americans United many times.

Long before the new Administration was sworn in its brain trust was at work on the troublesome school aid issue. It had received a directive to find a constitutional way to provide aid to religious schools that would not antagonize the Protestants. This seemed like a tall order but the Johnson team made it. At least they might have made it. Whether their formula is constitutional remains to be seen. That aside, however, they made an incredible success of it. The Catholic leadership was jubilant and Protestants who only a year or two before had been fighting aid to religious schools actually joined in a great cooperative endeavor to pass the legislation. Even some Baptist leaders declared that all church-state problems had been resolved in the Administration's proposal.

There were three keys to the legislative program which appeared to soften the fury of the religious issue. One was the old Catholic plea of "aid to the child." There would be no assistance to religious schools—only to the students in them. The next key was poverty. Not only would the legislation help children, it would help poor children. Here was a double-barreled appeal to all social welfare and humanitarian instincts of the clergy. How could one oppose a program designed to aid poor children? The third key was that of the special category. Aid to religious schools would not be for existing programs but for special programs with special purposes. It appeared, for example, that a teacher could not be hired with public funds to teach reading at a parochial school but he could be hired to teach remedial reading there. It was pointed out that the difference between remedial and nonremedial reading might be difficult to define, but that was the way it was.

The Elementary and Secondary Education Act of 1965 which is now law provides various kinds of aid for religious schools. Some of these forms of aid have nothing to do with the poverty situations to which the act was ostensibly pitched in the first instance. Libraries of religious schools can be stocked via loan for the life of the items. Mobile educational services as well as educational TV and radio are examples of the kind of assistance that can be provided along with salaries for teachers in certain kinds of subjects. Shared time or dual enrollment programs between public and religious schools receive enormous encouragement through a specific commitment to provide federal funds for their support. The flow of federal funds to such programs virtually assures the breakdown of state prohibitions against public aid to religious schools. Some states have actually passed enabling legislation so that the federal grants can be utilized. In other states the attorneys general have given approval, provided none of the state's funds are used—only federal money. The state constitution applies only to state funds!

THE JOHNSON CONSENSUS:
FEDERAL AID TO RELIGIOUS SCHOOLS

Basic to the legislation and the major triumph of the National Catholic Welfare Conference is the provision spelled out in specific terms that no funds can be expended on the public schools of any state until arrangements have been made for assistance to parochial schools—or rather, to students in parochial schools, as it is described. This had been insisted on by the Catholics to insure that they would get their "share" of any federal aid actually provided. Then there is the companion provision that in case state boards of education simply cannot cooperate in the federal aid program because of their own constitutional provisions, aid can be provided by the Federal Government directly to the religious schools. A final feature from which the Catholics expect a great deal in many urban situations is the plan for supplementary educational services to be arranged by a joint public-parochial school consortium in any community desiring it. These services can be provided in parochial as well as public schools.

The legislation contains one formal nod to church-state separation. Tacked on at the very end of the bill, it reads:

Nothing contained in this Act shall be construed to authorize the making of any payment under this Act, or under any Act amended by the Act, for religious worship or instruction.

There is no provision for enforcement of this stipulation. There is recognition of the fact that the various programs contemplated in the Act would channel support into religious schools which exist for the very purpose which the law solemnly professes not to aid. The sectarian disclaimer is a nod to separation of church and state but no more. Some called it a bad joke.

At this point it must be said that this was the formula that succeeded. It was not so much the formula—for it was, after all, rather transparent. It was President Johnson's success in lining up a consensus type of support for legislation that was acclaimed as improving the education of all the children, particularly those in poverty stricken areas.

The real tragedy of the bill as Americans United pointed out with tedious insistence was that it opened the door to achieve, step-by-step, full public subsidy to religious schools. Should this concept of school aid prevail, there would never again be a question as to whether federal funds should be used to assist religious schools. It would only be a question of how the assistance would be given and how much would be spent. As President Johnson himself remarked about the Elementary and Secondary Education Act of 1965: (This is) "just the beginning, the first giant stride."

Cardinal Spellman was pleased with the bill. The Catholic press was jubilant and hailed it as the first real official recognition of Catholic education. The Catholic leadership in the House, spearheaded by Rep. James J. Delaney from his key post on the Rules Committee, and Rep. Hugh L. Carey from his key post on the Education Subcommittee, and Rep. John W. McCormack from his position as Speaker of the House, pushed the bill with energy and enthusiasm. When the Catholic action group, Citizens for Educational Freedom, began to complain that the bill did not provide enough for denominational schools, the group's adviser, Father Virgil C. Blum, S.J., quickly straightened them out:

This is just the beginning of a vast Federal program aiding the education of children and is a good bill because it respects the principle that every child can and should share in Federal aid.[1]

The church-state issue was raised in the Congressional debates. Rep. Edith Green, ranking member of the House Education Subcommittee, expressed grave doubts about some of the church-state tie-ups envisaged.[2] Sen. Sam J. Ervin of North Carolina, the Senate's ablest constitutional lawyer, spoke to the issue with great eloquence. He pressed, as he had on other occasions, for an amendment providing for a prompt review before the Supreme Court of the constitutionality of the church-state provisions.[3] This was the last thing the Senate wanted. Nobody really listened. It was like trying to explain Einstein's relativity to pithecanthropus man. The great consensus was on. The legislation passed with comfortable margins in both chambers and was signed into law by President Johnson. It was only for $1.3 billion—a paltry sum as Congressional spending goes. But it was "only the beginning."

The American Civil Liberties Union saw church-state dangers in the legislation. The American Jewish Congress gave solemn warnings. Leo Pfeffer, perhaps the best known church-state lawyer in the United States, brilliantly presented the constitutional issue for the committees, showing that the plan to evade that issue was really not very ingenious and could not succeed.

Americans United gave the legislation its usual careful analysis. Our representatives appeared at one hearing after another, patiently analyzing, dissecting, interpreting the church-state issue.

I recall that in an appearance before a House Subcommittee on Education which was studying the aid bill proposed by the Administration, I bore down harder than one usually does on such occasions. I said bluntly:

THE JOHNSON CONSENSUS:
FEDERAL AID TO RELIGIOUS SCHOOLS

We understand the dilemma you face. We understand and appreciate the ecclesiastical pressures that for nearly 20 years, according to our own observations, have barred general Federal school aid proposals from passage. These pressures are mounted by one church and by one church only—a church that operates 95 per cent of the sectarian elementary schools and stands to draw 95 per cent of the sectarian allocations under this bill. We realize that this bill is born of a desperate desire to propose something that can pass. Gentlemen, the price being exacted here is too high. This bill will scuttle separation of church and state in the United States. I am a Methodist. This bill will mean that we in our Methodist Church will be paying in taxes for a part of the budget of the Catholic parish down the street.

All of this talk about aiding children, justice to parents, helping to cure poverty, and all the rest, should not obscure that basic fact. This is a tax for religion, however miniscule and, once on the books, it will be steadily increased as sectarian pressures mount. Whatever the pressures exerted here . . . I assure you that in the long run (this legislation) will establish arrangements the people will not welcome. This legislation does move toward a partial union of state and church with some contribution of government funds for church support. It is not just the facts that concern us; it is their direction. They point the wrong way. We believe that the increasing involvement of government with churches envisaged in these legislative proposals is socially destructive, filled with the promise of intercreedal strife and mutually bad for both church and state.

Some of the amendments proposed by us were actually incorporated into the bill. For example we urged that under Title III the funds for the supplementary centers should not be administered through the consortium of predominantly private school personnel but solely through public agencies. This was eventually done.

Yet we hoped against hope that some miracle would happen and that the questionable church-state provisions would be deleted. A predominantly Protestant group ourselves, we were almost alone in this hope. The National Association of Evangelicals did speak out against the church-state dangers of the bill. But the National Council of Churches joined the "consensus" for it. The old-line, denominational leadership followed suit. Legislation which even a decade before would have drawn cries of agony from men in the same positions now drew a chorus of approval, instead. Here was convincing evidence of the Protestant defection in church and state.

At the turn of the century the Protestant consensus for money line separation of church and state was as close to the point of unanimity as anything can ever get among Protestants. Many citizens of Roman Catholic faith were also sincere believers in the "American way" in church and state. The Jewish community was even more solidly separationist than the Protestants. The Protestant defection from the separationist position did not really begin until the 1950's—just about the time the Catholic bishops had determined to go for public subsidy.

It is curious that the defection among Protestants should have been confined almost exclusively to the extreme liberal wing of the church. (The Missouri Synod Lutheran defection came only after federal aid to religious schools had begun and its leaders were simply unable to resist the pressures of their own schoolmen for public funds.) At first it took the direction of a brotherhooder's sympathy for the underdog. "Catholics have rights, too, and we must respect their position."

During the early days of Americans United one of Glenn Archer's major problems was to convince the public that the Catholic hierarchy was really out for the parochial school subsidy. This was denied by the Catholics themselves when it seemed expedient, and the denial would be promptly echoed by brotherhood Protestants. When Cardinal Spellman suffered a hostile public reaction in a controversy with Mrs. Eleanor Roosevelt over aid for Catholic schools back in 1949, he quickly backed down on his demands and pleaded that he was only seeking a little money for "auxiliary services" to children in parochial schools.[4] It took him 10 years to get back to the demands he had made in the first place.

During those years it was customary whenever one alluded to Catholic demands for parochial school subsidy to have a young Protestant minister (usually from Union Theological Seminary, New York City) leap to his feet. Shaking with righteous indignation, he would state that Catholic leaders had made it abundantly clear that they were not seeking general public support for their schools—only a few fringe benefits. "We must be fair to our brothers," he would chide. If that kind of incident happened once it happened fifty times. What made the performance convincing was the fact that the young minister probably believed it himself. We no longer have that problem today, but while Protestant clergy were coddling themselves with that kind of thinking the Catholic leadership was preparing its offensive.

The ecumenical movement of the fifties and sixties contributed substantially to this Protestant defection. Catholic clergy started joining what had hitherto been Protestant ministerial groups. In Oklahoma, New Mexico, and Michigan there were instances of Catholic churches uniting with the Councils of Churches. In this way any effective opposition of such groups to government assistance to parochial schools was rendered impossible. The subject could not even be discussed.

THE JOHNSON CONSENSUS:
FEDERAL AID TO RELIGIOUS SCHOOLS

The first real breakthrough for Catholic Action in official Protestantism took place in February, 1964 when the Religious Liberty Department of the National Council of Churches held a meeting in Columbus, Ohio to formulate a strategy in regard to such church-state problems as that presented by school aid proposals. This was a Protestant meeting. Most Protestant groups in the United States were represented, either officially or unofficially. It was a Protestant meeting to formulate a Protestant church-state position. Yet, the sponsoring group, the National Council's Religious Liberty Department, invited a quota of Roman Catholic priests from the National Catholic Welfare Conference to be present. One of them was assigned to each section of the conference. They joined freely in the discussion, unabashedly pressed for the Catholic position, did everything but vote.

It is difficult to see what possible excuse there could have been for inviting Catholic priests to attend what was nothing in the world but an interior meeting of Protestants. But there they were and they exerted a strong influence on changing the National Council's position on school aid. Between them and the Protestant college administrators, aching for government money, the strict separationists had a little more than they could handle. Hammered at by these groups from the right and the left, the delegates finally passed a pronouncement which seriously changed the Council's traditional position opposing government aid to religious schools. The Conference declared that "government may legitimately support specific programs of church-affiliated health and welfare agencies" where a "clearly identifiable public interest . . ." is involved. Also that public funds may be appropriated for parochial schools "in support of specific programs conducted by such institutions to meet particular health and welfare needs."[5] A small concession that gave the entire case away! Msgr. George Higgins of the National Catholic Welfare Conference was jubilant. "The tone of this meeting," and document, he told the press, "is an indication that there will be possible in the future closer relationship and dialogue among Catholics and Protestants."[6]

Christianity and Crisis, a small journal on the extreme liberal edge of Protestantism, published at Union Theological Seminary in New York City, was an early advocate of Protestant withdrawal from strict separationism. This publication after repeatedly sniping at what it called the intransigence of Americans United, finally came out for some tax support of parochial schools. This it described as a "new approach" to the problem.[7] Methodist Bishop Fred Pierce Corson appointed a committee to establish Methodist schools in order to overcome "godlessness" in the public schools. He pleaded that the time may have come to provide some government assistance to religious schools.[8] As the controversy over federal aid to religious schools began to shape up nationally, President John Bennett of Union Theological Seminary remarked that "Many of us feel that what is good for the Roman Catholic Church is good for us. . . . Americans have to help all school children get an education and this means across-the-board aid for nonreligious instruction."[9] This was total capitulation.

The Protestant Episcopal Church broke with its traditional stand against government grants for church schools at its 61st General Convention meeting in 1964. In its official pronouncement on the subject the Convention amended its previous stand "by recognizing the propriety of including (private and parochial) schools in general public welfare programs such as the provision of standard textbooks and of equal bus transportation."[10]

When the Elementary and Secondary Act of 1965 was presented to Congress, the Administration was easily able to sell it to the old line Protestant leadership on the ground that it was really a welfare program to aid all poor children. Here are famous words of the "consensus." Dean M. Kelley, executive of the Religious Liberty Department, National Council of Churches:

Main Protestant bodies of the nation have found a common ground with Roman Catholics on which they can accept the President's proposal for federal aid to educationally deprived children.[11]

Arthur S. Flemming, vice-president of the National Council of Churches, favored the legislation in Congressional testimony as a "basically sound proposal."[12] Dr. H. B. Sissel, secretary for National Affairs of the United Presbyterian Church, USA, praised congressmen for a bill which "seeks to avoid placing the Congress . . . again on the horns of the old church-state dilemma. . . ."[13] Dr. C. Emanuel Carlson, executive of the Baptist Joint Committee on Public Affairs, stated that his reservations about the bill had been dissolved. "Most of the church-state issues in President Johnson's aid to education bill have been eliminated," he said.[14] The *Christian Century,* like the Laodicean Church in the Book of Revelation, blew neither hot nor cold and took no position. That probably meant that Kyle Haselden and Martin Marty were on opposite sides and they just decided to sit it out.

That left Americans United along with the National Association of Evangelicals, Jewish groups and the American Civil

Liberties Union to point to the towering church-state perils in the Elementary and Secondary Education Act of 1965.

A new factor had meanwhile entered into the controversy over public assistance to religious schools. This was the group called Citizens for Educational Freedom. This group founded by Judge Anthony D. Daly in St. Louis had a close affinity with the Jesuits of St. Louis University. Spiritual mentor of the CEF was a Jesuit priest on the faculty of Marquette University, Father Virgil C. Blum. The CEF bible was a book by Father Blum which explained how Congress could evade the constitutional strictures on aid to religious schools by a tuition grant or tax credit program for the benefit of parents. It was Father Blum's theory that if the grants were indirect, reaching the institution only after pausing a moment with the parent, that this would pass muster. Since the Supreme Court had time and time again enunciated the principle that what might not be done directly might not be done indirectly, either, the Blum thesis appeared absurd on the face. But it had considerable vogue among Catholic parents and even some Catholic lawyers.

CEF had been set up with the avowed purpose of combatting Americans United. Its organization was patterned rather closely on our own. Originally the group had considerable more noise than skill and must have been a trial to its Jesuit tutors. Jesuit priests actually wrote much of the material for CEF and directed its effort. I recall one amusing episode in this connection. One day I noticed a new pamphlet being distributed by CEF called "The Battle for Children's Minds." It was a slick job and clearly showed the Jesuit touch. What got me about it, though, was the name of the author—John Brewster. This was overdone. There was just too much of old Protestant New England about that name. I determined to find out just who John Brewster was. My hunch was right. John Brewster turned out to be a Jesuit priest, Father H. O. H. Walker, of the Sociology Department at St. Louis University.

Under Jesuit tutelage the CEF became a more effective instrument of clerical action. It did touch the Congressional scene lightly but that arena was left for the most part to the National Catholic Welfare Conference. The real theater of action for CEF was in the states. Here it sought a number of objectives—changes in state constitutions so as to permit aid to religious schools, parochial bus laws, parochial textbook laws, services to parochial school students, and, of course, the tuition grant or tax certificate aid.

CEF was an outright political group, in some ways the American counterpart of the various Catholic political parties of

Europe and Latin America. It played for keeps. If legislators failed to vote on parochial school aid as it thought they should, CEF would organize to encompass their defeat in the next election. Thus, in 1964 the CEF sought to wreak political reprisal in Pennsylvania on Senators Henry J. Propert, Marvin V. Keller and Paul L. Wagner, all of whom had once opposed a parochial bus bill in the Legislature. These efforts failed more often than they succeeded but it was the kind of situation every politician avoids like the plague. The CEF could be rough. Sometimes it advocated the "dumping" of children from parochial schools into public schools if demands for parochial school aid were not met. In Kentucky the CEF announced that it would carry out in that state the same tactics that Cardinal Spellman and the Catholic Welfare Conference had used with Congress. CEF announced that it had enough members "to defeat any legislation that excludes us."[15] The pronouncement was aimed at a special session of the Kentucky Legislature which had been called to deal with crisis needs in the schools. Gerald J. McGee stated that if additional taxes were provided for Jefferson County schools his group would start a move for a recall referendum. McGee charged that Catholic parents were being deprived of their constitutional rights because their children did not benefit from school taxes. Two years earlier CEF made a losing effort to amend the Kentucky Constitution so as to permit use of tax funds for the support of parochial schools.

In the 1962 Congressional election in New York City, CEF sold a Catholic Republican candidate, Thomas Galvin, on the idea of campaigning for public funds for parochial schools. His Jewish opponent on the Democratic ticket, Ben Rosenthal, supported President Kennedy's position on the matter. Rosenthal squeaked through by 193 votes in a solid Democratic district. The clamant Citizens took full credit for Galvin's strong run. Mark Murphy, CEF director in Queens-Brooklyn, said: "We're encouraged. We're going to be a factor in every statewide and Federal race from now on . . ."[16]

Low tactics were frequently favored by CEF. The group gave wide distribution to a story from the *Times Review* of La Crosse, Wis., October 8, 1959 which was headlined: "No Bus For Catholic Students—Mother and Six Children Die." The story was an inflammatory one seeking to arouse public opinion against those who would not favor the use of public funds to transport children to religious schools. No mention was made in the story of the Catholic bishops whose rule forbade Catholic parents to patronize the public schools and the buses serving them.

In Wisconsin, Supreme Court justices are elected by popular vote. In the 1964 election CEF sought to obtain commitments from the candidates for these posts that they would agree to reverse a recent decision of the Court which held that free transportation to religious schools was unconstitutional in Wisconsin. This one was too much for the *Milwaukee Journal* which worked the Citizens over in a scathing editorial.[17]

One of the basic ground rules which the Jesuits insisted on was that CEF should present itself to the public not as a Catholic organization but as a combined effort of all faiths believing in public assistance to religious schools. Some Protestants were, in fact, found who were willing to front for CEF, but they were never more than a corporal's guard. The group was and is Catholic, despite all its public disclaimers. At first the bishops were a bit nervous about CEF lest its aggressiveness stir an anticlerical reaction. As the Citizens continued their strident campaigns and the public did not become aroused, the bishops began to reassess their earlier skepticism. With a parochial bus battle coming up in Pennsylvania, the Philadelphia archdiocese realized that CEF could make a real contribution in the political slugging. Accordingly, the diocese gave a formal endorsement of CEF.[18] CEF was also endorsed by the Knights of Columbus in Missouri and Ohio, the Missouri endorsement carrying also a pledge to merge the Knights' political action with that of CEF.[19] Dale Francis, a well known Catholic actionist and author of "Operation Understanding" was permitted to publish a half-page appeal for CEF membership in the popular national Catholic newspaper *Our Sunday Visitor.* Memberships were announced as $1 for individuals, $2 for families, and $10 for contributors. "Do something about it now," Francis wrote.

School aid had become the major concern of Catholic action. Some Protestant leadership under the aegis of the ecumenical movement, was providing assistance. The prospective annual flow of some $2½ billion into church coffers to sustain Catholic denominational schools would have many of the practical effects of a religious establishment. For aid to a church school is aid to the church which controls it. Nothing is surer once such a process has commenced than that one thing will lead to another. Some aid always becomes more aid. More begets more because church officialdom becomes involved with government officialdom and the one manipulates the other.

Protestants will, of course, get into this political game. They are already commencing to do so. But their chances in a competition of this kind are less than hopeless. For one thing, their structure is all wrong. Their free, democratic procedures are not at all designed for the scramble. Nor are they equipped to hold their own in the struggle against control of the state over their institutions. Every Protestant official with whom I ever discussed the question of public assistance to church institutions was deathly afraid of public controls. The typical Protestant institutional head wants public funds without public controls. The fear of controls worries him to death. Catholic officials, on the other hand, are not nearly so concerned about this. They have had centuries of experience in getting their funds from the state and avoiding state controls at the same time. They figure that they can control the controllers. Their fundamental advantage is that they have a system for it. Their tight, authoritarian control gives them a mobility of action, makes possible the quick shift, the evasive maneuver. Here is a kind of competition which Protestants are bound to lose.

In the controversy over government aid to religious schools Catholic Action enjoyed one considerable advantage. It had the ready availability of all the news media to bring its case before the public. I have repeatedly been amazed at the microscopic events scheduled by CEF or an archdiocesan group which would draw publicity entirely out of proportion to the event itself. When we stated our position on school aid at a public meeting the press would frequently call some local prelate and get the "Catholic reply" to our position. The reply would receive more prominence than our original statement.

The most childish and trite Catholic arguments for public aid to denominational schools would receive extensive treatment in the press. Our careful, constitutional and moral analysis of the problem would be totally ignored. In reporting our national conference the press would frequently give more space to the attacks on us made by some local cleric than to the program of the conference. All this was because the Catholics enjoyed a built-in propaganda advantage. They stood as a potential threat to the press of which the press was never unaware. They presented an imposing image of solidarity. Our support was diffused and posed no implicit threat to anybody.

With politicians it was the same. The practice of "listening to the Catholics" in matters of legislation has become almost universal among them because they feel the Catholics are in position to "do something" for or to them. Protestants will not do anything for or to them. Nor will other religious segments of the community.

The result of all this was that Catholic Action had a large opportunity at the American public in contrast with our small opportunity. Wrapping about themselves the robes of religious reverence, presenting themselves as the champions of God and piety, the Catholic leaders pursued their self-seeking campaign with enormous success. They actually began to have an effect on public opinion, softening it for their final triumph.

There remains, however, one huge imponderable which may decisively affect the outcome of the struggle. This is the possibility of anticlericalism, a possibility which may well give all religious leaders pause. The Roman Catholic drive for tax support of its denominational schools is a classic in clerical action. It is an obvious exercise in wresting political control, then exploiting that control to derive tax support for its enterprise. Historically, such an operation has never been consummated without a reaction. Clericalism has always bred anticlericalism. The unchurched, together with millions of those nominally associated with the church, will turn against the church's officialdom. When this reaction develops it will be directed not against the Roman Catholic Church as such, though that church will be its primary objective. It will be directed against the entire religious enterprise.

A religious enterprise which draws its support from taxes, battles competitive groups for tax funds and tax advantage, and presents an image of secular pursuit and concern, will not attract people to its spiritual mission. It will, rather, repel them. It will burden them with the disillusionment of those who look to the church for something better but find there the old sick secularism with which they are all too familiar. The churches and the clergy have always enjoyed a high degree of popularity in this country. There has hardly ever been a whisper of anticlericalism. Churches were looked upon with favor and religion was considered a good thing. The coming of government subsidy of religion with all its accompanying phenomena will create a new psychology at this point. It may lead us into the first era of antichurch feeling this young nation has ever known. In such an era the people will come to a new appreciation of the separation of church and state.

[1] *Church and State*, May, 1965.

[2] *Washington Post*, March 20, 1965.

[3] *Congressional Record*, April 9, 1965, page 7344.

[4] *Church and State in the United States*, Stokes and Pfeffer, Harper & Row, New York City (1964), page 440.

[5] Report of the National Conference on Church and State Sponsored by the Department of Religious Liberty, National Council of Churches of Christ in America, Columbus, Ohio, February 4-7, 1964.

[6] *Detroit Free Press*, February 8, 1964.

[7] *Christianity and Crisis*, October 28, 1963.

[8] *Christian Century*, November 6, 1963.

[9] *Church and State*, May, 1965.

[10] *Tablet*, October 29, 1964.

[11] *Ibid, February 25, 1965.*

[12] *Church Herald*, February 19, 1965.

[13] Statement of H. B. Sissel, Sec. for National Affairs of the United Presbyterian Church at Hearings before the Senate Subcommittee on Education on S. 370, Part 5, page 2888.

[14] *Baptist Public Affairs News Service*, February 9, 1965.

[15] *Louisville Courier-Journal*, June 3, 1965.

[16] *Church and State*, May, 1962.

[17] Ibid, March, 1963.

[18] *Catholic Standard and Times*, August 14, 1964.

[19] *Church and State*, November, 1964.

Typical
"captive school"
classroom
in Kentucky, 1956.

chapter # VIII IN THE COURTS

Americans United was conceived by its founders as an educational and legal group. Considerable litigation in the church-state field was envisaged. Decisions of the United States Supreme Court concerning bus transportation to religious schools, textbooks for students in religious schools and public assistance to sectarian hospitals had already dramatized the importance of the courts in the church-state struggle. The choice of the dean of a law school to head Americans United was a deliberate one. The founders wanted someone with courtroom experience and versed in legal theory as well. The courts might well be the last bastion of defense for separation of church and state. Americans United must be equipped to play its part in this significant area.

The litigation techniques of Americans United were developed by Glenn Archer during the early years of the movement and have remained much the same ever since. We have frequently been charged as being "trouble makers." The inference is that we go into communities and raise church-state problems, setting group against group. There is not a scintilla of truth in the charge. Indeed, the exact opposite is the truth. We have often been the catalyst of mediation and agreement. Or, failing this, we have supported local citizens in seeking legal adjudication of the points in controversy.

We have never gone into a community and created a controversy. The controversy was there first; then we were called in to help. This was the invariable procedure. We have never gone into a community unless we were invited in by responsible citizens. Having been thus duly invited, the organization would dispatch a representative to make an investigation of the facts. The next step would be to bring the conflicting groups together, if possible, to advise as to the legal situation, and then to seek an agreement that would resolve the problems. Many times the mere presence of a POAU attorney in the community would itself hasten resolution of the difficulty. But where no agreement was possible and the situation called for litigation, the organization would then support plaintiffs in a court action. Local counsel was always retained. Counsel did not supply their services gratis but were always paid suitable fees, in part from local funds and in part by Americans United.

The early legal reputation of Americans United was established in "captive school" suits. A captive school is a public school that has been taken over by a sectarian group and operated for its sectarian purposes. The only survey of captive schools in the United States was made by Americans United in 1959. It indicated that such institutions existed in 22 states. There were some 2,055 religious—nuns, brothers, priests—on the payroll as teachers and administrators. Chief, and virtually sole offender, was the Roman Catholic Church. Captive schools were and are generally found in isolated or rural communities with a large Catholic population. The captive school was a device to avoid paying for two schools in a community that found it difficult to foot the bills. The plan was simply to iron the Catholic school into the public school and operate both as a single package. The school would remain Catholic in instruction and management but its bills would be paid from public taxes. Such a school would characteristically have two listings—one in the Roman Catholic School Directory as a parish school of that denomination, and another in the public school directory of the state as a public institution.

The usual procedure would be for a church-oriented public school board to turn over instruction arrangements to the local priest. He would contract with one of the many Catholic religious orders to supply teaching nuns for the school. These nuns do not teach free as they do in regular Catholic schools. They are paid regular public school salaries. Since they are under a vow of poverty, however, they simply sign over their checks to the head of their own order or to the local bishop. There is no income tax deduction because of the poverty vow and the entire sum goes to their church.

Antonito, Colorado is a typical captive school situation. It began in the early thirties when local taxes could not provide enough to keep the public schools in operation. The Catholic Benedictine order came forward and offered to staff the two public schools with teachers at a considerably lower figure than the board had been paying. It seemed like a good solution since most of the people were Catholic anyway. Times eventually got better. The opening of three perlite mines in the area brought new families to the community. They were unhappy that the public schools were in fact parochial schools and objected to them. Most preferred to live elsewhere and drive considerable distances to work.

Some indication of the nature of the Antonito schools can be derived from the listing of the new teachers for the public system in the *Antonito Ledger-News*. This list included:

Sister Bernice, superintendent of Antonito schools; Sister Arsenia, high school principal; Sister Huberta, librarian and office secretary; Sister Alice Marie, science and mathematics teacher, Sister Pauline, in charge of National Defense Education Act requisitions and teaching of Spanish.[1]

Thirty-six of the thirty-seven teachers in the Antonito public schools that year were Catholic and 26 of the 37 were sisters of the Order of St. Benedict.

In the typical captive school instruction in catechism is offered in the classrooms. If there is some static from Protestants or others the instruction may be scheduled before or after school hours. All instruction is supplied by Catholic nun teachers clad in the distinctive garb of their religious order. The classrooms are adorned with religious statues and other indicia of the Catholic faith. Mass is held in association with the school program (usually in an adjacent church) and children are marched to and from the religious service.

Some years ago Americans United produced a film, "Captured," to educate the public in regard to captive schools. The film was carefully prepared and its documentation was impeccable. The fact is that we eliminated some of the more objectionable items from the film even though they were strictly factual in order that no sensibilities would be offended. The film was violently attacked by the Catholics, nevertheless, and some Protestants wrote us that we ought to be ashamed of ourselves for such a bigoted attack on the Catholic Church! All the film did was to depict situations which actually obtain in hundreds of American communities. Should not some criticism attach itself to the people who are responsible for these conditions as well as to those who merely depict them?

Typical of the feelings of Protestants and others languishing in a community with captive schools is this letter from an anonymous resident of Antonito:

As a Protestant minority here in Antonito, we plead with others who share the responsibility of guarding our precious heritage of religious freedom, to demand such legislation in our state, as shall ensure the protection of our public schools from such manipulation as prevails in our town.[2]

Alas! The remedy was not legislative. The legislative intent was already clear. The Antonito schools were in violation of the state's laws and its constitution. The only recourse was that of litigation. Eventually there was a call from beleaguered citizens to Americans United in Washington, D. C. The original investigation in Antonito, Colorado was done by Glenn Archer himself. He conferred with all interested parties in the community. He reported that even one of the Catholic lay teachers complained about the school, describing it as a "cathechism school." A long discussion with the local priest appeared to make headway. He agreed to review the situation. New arrangements for the Antonito schools were in prospect until Gov. McNichols, campaigning for reelection, made a speech in the Antonito school. He praised the nuns as being the finest kind of public school teachers. The priest took this as an endorsement of the local school arrangements and hardened his position from that moment. Apparently a lawsuit will be the only way to restore the local schools to public management and control.

Will there be a lawsuit? On two occasions local citizens had appealed for assistance to Americans United. On both occasions we promptly responded, conducted an investigation and promised our support in a suit. At the zero hour the plaintiffs have indicated reluctance. The illegal sectarian domination of the Antonito schools will likely continue without interruption unless concerned citizens bury their fears and take action. When they are ready we shall be ready.

Captive schools have long enjoyed official Catholic support. One of the specific concerns of the Legal Department of the National Catholic Welfare Conference is to resist "challenges to religious employed as teachers in public schools."[3]

Largest remaining nests of captive schools are in Indiana, Ohio, Illinois and Kansas, though a troublesome situation in Hays, Kansas was set in process of adjustment with Americans United participating. There are a number in Ohio being challenged by Americans United in a Mercer County suit, and anywhere from one to a dozen in 19 other states. In 1948, however, New Mexico and Missouri were by far the worst situations. The first important litigations supported by Americans United were captive school lawsuits in those states. The very first issue of *Church and State* published May 15, 1948 called attention to:

IN THE COURTS

*New Mexico's sad plight where 139 nuns and brothers and
one priest are being paid by the state as teachers in the public
schools . . . POAU has aided in the moves to close this breach
through legal counsel.*

The violations in the New Mexico schools were so numerous
and widespread as to create almost a pattern of defiance of the
law. The schools of Carrizozo, Socorro, Belen, San Fidel,
Cubero, Cuba, Bernalillo, Pena Blanca, Waterflow, Blanco,
Lumberton, Parkview, Tierra Amarilla, Abiquiu, San Juan,
Pecos, Santa Cruz, Penasco, Costilla, Villanueva, Ribera, Mora,
Old Las Vegas, Ranchos de Taos, and Dixon were among those
about which specific complaints had been lodged by persons
of minority faiths. The objections all pointed to the fact the
Roman Catholic faith was being forced upon all children in
these quasi public schools of New Mexico. It seemed evident
that if some move were not promptly made the Catholic clergy
was in a fair way to infiltrate and capture the entire public
school system of the state.

When Glenn Archer arrived in Washington to assume direction of POAU, the acting Director J. M. Dawson had already
received appeals for assistance from New Mexico and had
retained the well-known constitutional lawyer E. Hilton Jackson
to assist in the matter. The counsel retained for the actual
handling of the case in the New Mexico Court was Judge Harry
L. Bigbee. Glenn Archer quickly entered the New Mexico situation, advised and assisted in preparation of the case and sat
with Mr. Bigbee during the conduct of the trial. Much of the
credit for the solid preparation which made possible the eventual success of the lawsuit must go to a Presbyterian minister,
the Rev. Paul Stevens. Stevens gathered voluminous evidence of
violations of law in many schools. This exhaustive factual record
was invaluable in winning the case. An occasional violation
here and there might have been condoned, but the accumula-
tion of evidence assembled by Mr. Stevens and Mr. Bigbee was
overwhelming. In all, 30 schools in 11 counties were specifically
involved in the lawsuit, *Zellers vs. Huff,*[4] which was brought
by 28 plaintiffs against more than 200 defendants. The suit was
brought in 1948. More than $600,000 in public funds flowed
annually to the Catholic Church in the form of salaries for the
teaching nuns.

Scores of New Mexico schools exhibited all the marks of
captive schools as described above and often some additional
ones as well. Happenings in the town of Dixon were especially
reprehensible. It was suddenly announced one day that the
public school had been closed and that all parents must send
their children to the Roman Catholic school which stood imme-

diately adjacent to the Catholic Church. The teaching in the school was done by members of a religious order, the Sisters of St. Francis. The only layman on the staff was a man who had been educated for the priesthood at Notre Dame. The Franciscan Order is not a teaching order and its members were not qualified to teach. Most of the sisters were German refugees who could not even speak intelligible English. A fine new public school building erected with WPA funds was abandoned and allowed to go to ruin.

Religious groups represented in the Dixon school were Catholic, Presbyterian, Pentecostal, Adventist, and Mormon. The Sisters required all children to say the "Hail Mary" four times a day. Buses were supposed to deliver the children for 9 A.M. classes but started bringing them as early as 7 and 7:30 in order to have all on hand for Mass at 8:30. Protestants could go to Mass or stand around outside until school opened at 9 o'clock. Special recognition and awards were given to those who mastered the Catholic catechism which was taught in the classroom. Classes were dismissed a half hour early every Thursday and Friday during Lent so that students could go to confession.

The people of Dixon raised $13,000 to build a new school where the first five grades could be taught by lay teachers, a genuine public school. But the day the school opened the board announced that it would have a Catholic nun for principal and several nuns as teachers. Alarmed at the furor, Archbishop Edwin V. Byrne of Santa Fe wrote a pastoral letter requesting that "no religious instruction be given in public school buildings by the (nun) teachers on school days. . . . "

This eased the situation to a certain extent in the captive schools of New Mexico but such an attempted adjustment could not correct a basically improper arrangement. There remained a great deal of sectarian intrusion in the schools and those committed to the teaching of their religion too easily reverted to their previous practices. It was at this point that an appeal for help was addressed to the fledgling Protestants and Other Americans United for Separation of Church and State.

The decision eventually handed down by District Judge E. Turner Hensley in March, 1949 sustained virtually all the POAU contentions. One hundred thirty nine members of Catholic religious orders were eliminated from the public payroll. Among the practices which the judge ordered to be terminated were:

Renting, leasing or acquiring by local or state school of any space for public school classes not under the complete control of the state.

Free bus transportation for students in parochial schools.
Purchase of textbooks for parochial schools and purchase of books especially for Roman Catholic schools.
Teaching of sectarian doctrine in any tax-supported schools.
Holding of public school classes in rooms where religious or sectarian symbols are displayed.
Payment of persons teaching sectarian doctrines.

Editorializing on the New Mexico outcome, *Church and State* commented:

The transition from the existing church-monopoly of the schools to a democratic system is going to be somewhat painful for the New Mexico authorities, because they had allowed themselves to be so thoroughly yoked by the parochial system.[5]

This was certainly the case. The state administration under the leadership of Attorney General Joe L. Martinez immediately took an obstructionist line and sought to frustrate the court's findings. The attorney general ruled, for example, that while textbooks could not be provided for religious schools, they could be provided to students in religious schools. Judge Hensley had ordered an end to the purchase or rent of church facilities for the conduct of public school classes. The practice of turning public school property over to Catholic authorities for conversion into parochial schools continued however. Completely dissatisfied with the outcome the plaintiffs, though they had been victorious in the lower court, felt it necessary to appeal to the New Mexico Supreme Court. The high court eventually heard the case and announced its finding in the fall of 1951.

A unanimous court upheld all principal points in Judge Hensley's decision. Justice James McGhee, speaking for the court, specifically barred 124 nuns and brothers from the public schools, while clearing 15 others because "there was no evidence to support a finding that they taught religion."[6] The Supreme Court also upheld the barring of public school classes from church-owned buildings, and the ban on transportation of parochial school pupils at public expense and the distribution of free textbooks to parochial schools. Justice McGhee commented on the use of religious as public school teachers:

We are not unmindful that members of the religious have served as teachers and have in the past rendered fine service. The fact that they were teaching religion in the public schools in violation of the state and federal constitutions was well known to school authorities, both local and state—by them condoned and in many cases encouraged.[7]

The Supreme Court held, however, that if members of religious orders did not wear their distinctive garb and did not offer sectarian teaching in the classroom, there was no objection to their serving as teachers in the public schools. In the spring of 1951, two years after the decision in the District Court, Archbishop Edwin F. Byrne of the Santa Fe, New Mexico Catholic diocese, announced that nuns and brothers teaching in the New Mexico public schools would not renew their contracts for the next school year.

While it is impossible to dwell upon or even mention the plethora of legal skirmishes in which Americans United was involved during the course of nearly two decades, some attention should assuredly be given to the famous Missouri school case of the early 1950's. Missouri was the second situation in which there had been a substantial takeover of public schools by the Roman Catholic leadership. Some 18 counties were involved with schools enrolling thousands of students and an annual flow of tax funds via teaching nuns to the Roman Catholic Church of at least $350,000.

After repeated calls for help, Glenn Archer visited St. Louis for a meeting with local leaders in the fall of 1950. Present at the meeting were John C. Mayne, a Council of Churches official who was later to become director of organization for POAU, William B. Massey, an official of the Scottish Rite Masons, Harry Avery, a local attorney, and Professor Pollard of the Concordia Lutheran Seminary. Here plans were laid for the Missouri school case—or for two cases, rather, because it was deemed advisable to separate the transportation issue and bring that in a second suit.

A local law firm was retained to represent a host of plaintiffs who had indicated their determination to press the issue in the Missouri court. Sponsoring the lawsuit in Missouri and assisting in the fund raising campaign was the Missouri Association for Free Public Schools, an affiliate of Americans United. The law firm originally chosen began to feel the effects of Catholic pressure and asked to be released from the case. At this point Judge Boyle Clark of Columbia was approached and he agreed to take the case. The choice proved to be an admirable one.

Glenn Archer was the architect of the Missouri schools case, *Berghorn v. Franklin County School District.*[8] The suit resulted in a smashing victory for the plaintiffs and preserved separation of church and state in Missouri for a generation or more. Indefatigable in the preparations for the suit was the director of organization for Americans United, John C. Mayne, a long time resident of Missouri. Judge Clark paid tribute to Mr. Mayne for his leadership of the Missouri Free Schools Association.

The New Mexico experience stood Archer in good stead. He knew now exactly the evidence that was needed and how to get it. One of the interesting issues of the suit was the legality of uniformed Catholic nuns as teachers in the public schools of Missouri. There could, of course, be no "religious test" for public school teachers. A Catholic would have the same right to a teaching post as a Presbyterian or a Methodist. But the plaintiffs argued that the Catholic teaching nun was a special kind of Catholic under a discipline that disqualified her for service in a free, public school. Of obvious relevance was the obligation of total obedience taken by the religious when they were admitted to the orders which were the Poor Sisters of Notre Dame, and the Sisters of the Adoration of the Most Precious Blood of O'Fallon.

There was great reluctance on the part of the Catholic bishop to disclose the oath. Finally, under threat of subpoena, he did produce the text. On the basis of it Judge Emmett J. Crouse held in his decree handed down April 21, 1952:

> *The Court further finds that upon admission to the respective orders the nuns who become members thereof, take stringent vows of obedience, poverty and chastity, that said nuns and each of them by virtue of their oaths of obedience place exclusive control over their personal actions in the hands of Church authorities and their superiors in their religious orders; that by virtue of their oaths of poverty said nuns and each of them renounce their civil, economic and secular beings; that by the very nature of the obligations of their oaths of obedience, said nuns, and each of them, place themselves beyond the control of civil authorities (except where agreeable to their superiors); that said nuns, and each of them, by their oaths cease to exist as free citizens and as individual economic units, and during their service execute contracts, receive and pay out money in taxes only in a nominal, perfunctory and formal sense, while, in reality, acting as instruments of their religious orders, engage in executing the policies of the Roman Catholic Church; that by the very nature of their obligations and of the control of the secular or sectarian existence and personal actions of the nuns. . . . is vested in the church authorities; that because of the character of their obligations said nuns are disqualified from teaching in any public school in the State of Missouri.*[9]

There were other findings of considerable church-state interest. The court held that:

> *. . . the policy of the State of Missouri with respect to separation of church and state in the public educational system of Missouri is so different from the policy of the Roman Catholic Church toward the desirability of the combination of religious and secular education, that said policies of the State of Missouri and of the Roman Catholic Church cannot be effectuated in any*

single school at the same time. The said policies are utterly inconsistent and mutually exclusive.[10]

The court held further that "wherever the policy of the Roman Catholic Church is, in effect, wholly and partially in any school, that school cannot in fact be a free public school within the meaning of the policy of the State of Missouri . . . "[11] Also that the use of any public monies, whether from local or state sources, "for the support of an alleged free public school in which the effectuation of church policies is either dominant or effective, is an unlawful act contrary to the declared policy and law of the State.[12]

The court sustained the plaintiffs on many related issues which had painted the composite picture of school systems under the total domination of a church. The hiring of Catholic nuns through a cleric or through the Mother Superior of a religious order, the juxtaposition of church and school in the "captive" arrangements, the wearing of a distinctive religious garb and distinctive religious symbols by the nun teachers, the display of distinctive religious symbols upon and within the school buildings, closing of school on Catholic religious holidays, intermingling of church and school functions, and sectarian instruction in the classroom—all were held to be in violation of Missouri law. The Missouri case is unique in that the court actually incorporated the entire history and Canon Law of the Roman Catholic Church into the opinion, using this as background and basis for the eventual findings.

Judge Crouse's opinion in *Berghorn v. Franklin County School District* was the most comprehensive ever rendered on church-state issues in a school case. The suit was brought on the ground that both the Missouri and Federal Constitutions had been violated by school practices within the state. The opinion of Judge Crouse unanimously sustained by the Supreme Court was not appealed by the defendants to the United States Supreme Court. In retrospect such an appeal might seem to have been desirable. For *Berghorn v. Franklin County School District* probes far more deeply into the church-state issue in schools than *Schempp-Murray, Engel, Zorach, McCollum* or *Everson.* Most of these cases dealt with a single item such as bus transportation or Bible reading. The comprehensive scope of *Berghorn* is made clear by the assertion of the Missouri Supreme Court in sustaining Judge Crouse that what the court had to consider was "the total effect of all the facts and circumstances in evidence in determining whether the schools in question are in fact free public schools."[13]

The Missouri Supreme Court went on to say, in a unanimous opinion, that "we need only refer to the agreed facts concerning the schools" and that on the basis of

these and other facts shown by this record, we think the conclusion is inescapable that these schools as maintained and operated by defendant District 8 and its officers at Gildehaus and Krakow, were in fact "controlled in the main by members of recognized orders of the Roman Catholic Church and by officials thereof," that such schools to a great degree were "managed and administered in a manner to promote the interests and policies of the Roman Catholic Church and of adherents of the Roman Catholic faith." [14]

The opinion then closes with the finding "that said schools were not in fact free public schools and were not entitled to be supported by public school money or public funds."

There remained the matter of bus transportation at public expense to religious schools. There the Circuit Court opinion of Judge R. B. Oliver III had favored the defendants and the plaintiffs had appealed to the Missouri Supreme Court. The high court in a unanimous opinion reversed Judge Oliver, finding that

We must and do hold that the public school funds used to transport the pupils part way to and from the St. Dennis Catholic School at Benton are not used for the purpose of maintaining free public schools and that such use of said funds is unlawful. [15]

The Missouri case set the pattern for all other captive school cases supported by Americans United. This suit demonstrated that if the evidence could be carefully gathered and effectively presented to an impartial court, captive school arrangements simply could not stand up. Some of the cases like those of Garden Plain, Kansas and Bremond, Texas were declared moot on the eve of trial because the defendants knew they were beaten and hastily corrected the sectarian abuses in the schools. Where the cases went to trial as in *Outcault v. Fleming Board of Education* (Colorado) and the famous Johnsburg, Illinois and Bradfordsville, Kentucky school cases, Americans United consistently prevailed.

The Bradfordsville, Kentucky case which began in 1954 was notable for the feelings it aroused as evidenced in a year-long school strike by parents, something unheard of in these days. Also for the virtual destruction of a community which resulted from the unwise policies of a sectarian dominated school board and superintendent. Under the plea of "consolidation" the Catholic Superintendent of Schools, Hugh C. Spalding, and the Marion County school board had systematically starved the high school in the predominantly Protestant end of the county while as systematically nourishing and building up a high school in the predominantly Catholic end of the county which was staffed largely with Catholic nun teachers. Residents of the Protestant community of Bradfordsville realized that with the closing of their school they would have to send their children to St. Charles or St. Francis schools to be taught by Roman Catholic nuns or to the independent school in Lebanon. They objected to the nun teachers at the two schools and quite as strenuously to Lebanon which they claimed was not a suitable place for their children to be educated. Eventually the board did close the Bradfordsville school and there was a disastrous school strike lasting an entire year.[16]

By the time Americans United was called in the situation was beyond negotiation. Superintendent Spalding refused any compromise and resolutely carried through the closing as scheduled. Two lawsuits were the result. One of the suits challenged the legality of expending public funds for salaries of Catholic nuns as teachers in the schools of Kentucky. The other asked that the state desist from payments to the Marion County Board of Education until it would halt illegal and discriminatory practices against Bradfordsville. Principal plaintiff was the Rev. James C. Rawlings, a retired Methodist minister, a resident of Marion County whose appeal for help brought Glenn Archer to Bradfordsville on a hot afternoon in the summer of 1953.

The suit to eliminate the nuns as public school teachers was initiated by the Kentucky Free Public Schools Committee, an Americans United affiliate, against the advice of Glenn Archer. He recognized the civil rights issue involved and the heavy burden to be carried. New Mexico and Missouri had taught him the strength of the composite case, the weakness of the isolated issue. If there were a single school practice that did not quite pass muster, the courts were reluctant to intervene. Considerable latitude in arrangements is given to local boards of education under our system. But if one could show a consistent pattern of sectarian encroachment and preemption of a school with any number of conspicuous sectarian practices going on, this was a different matter. The attorney in the nun-teacher suit, Eugene Siler, later a Congressman from Kentucky, believed very strongly in bringing the suit on the issue of the religious garb only. He brought the suit on that single issue and it was lost in the Kentucky Court of Appeals. Mr. Siler argued that Catholic sisters "religiously robed and religiously named and religiously dedicated to their own Roman

Catholic Church, are completely out of place in Kentucky free public schools which are supported by public taxes of Catholics, Jews, Protestants, Baptists, pagans, and other American citizens."[17] But a divided Court of Appeals in an opinion handed down in February, 1955 rejected his reasoning and upheld Circuit Court Judge William B. Ardery in his decision that the garbed nuns could not be barred as public school teachers. The case was not appealed to the United States Supreme Court.

For the other case Jesse K. Lewis of Lexington, Kentucky was engaged. He pressed the case with great vigor and his success in the Court of Appeals made him a well known figure in the state.

The carefully gathered evidence showed that the Catholic dominated school board of Marion County had been contracting with the Roman Catholic Church for years for school buildings, that more than 40 nuns were engaged to teach in six schools, that they were employed under their religious names, served under their religious discipline, wore their religious garbs and emblems while teaching.[18] After the deduction of a small stipend for living expenses the remainder of the nuns' salaries was turned over to their order. The county superintendent did deduct the federal income tax from the nuns' salaries but the money was returned to them later and they gave it to their order. Nuns and priests of the Catholic Church offered sectarian instruction in the classrooms during school hours and offered an additional one hour of formal religious instruction in the Catholic Church next door. Classes were dismissed on Catholic holy days. The schools were rife with sectarian symbols and sectarian periodicals and books.

In a unanimous opinion handed down June 22, 1956 the Kentucky Court of Appeals ordered the Marion County Board of Education to:

(1) *Stop violating the state law that forbids sectarian books and literature to be distributed in the common schools.*

(2) *Stop keeping sectarian periodicals in and about the libraries of the county schools.*

(3) *Stop spending public school funds for religious or sectarian purposes.*

(4) *Stop the practice of halting school bus runs on Catholic religious holidays that are not also legal state or national holidays.*[19]

In regard to the touchy issue of the location of the schools the court held:

We direct the Circuit Court to issue an injunction requiring the County Board of Education and the superintendent of county schools, as soon as is practicable, to establish a high school system that will afford all children in the county equal educational opportunity.

So long as the Board of Education chooses to continue a system of regional or area high schools, compliance with the injunction will require re-establishment of a four-year high school in the eastern section of the county.

However, the board will have the alternative of compliance by establishing a system based on a centrally located county high school.

Sometime after both decisions had been rendered I happened to encounter one of the justices of the Court of Appeals at a social occasion. In discussing the cases he remarked: "We were unwilling to bar these women as public school teachers merely because of their religious faith and commitment. But when we saw what was actually going on in these classrooms that was a different story. We knew something had to be done."

The aftermath of the Bradfordsville case is enlightening. The Court of Appeals gave the Marion County Board two clear alternatives: the board could reopen the Bradfordsville school or it could establish one central school to serve the entire area. It never did either one. The next decade provided the perfect demonstration of school officials who were determined not to comply with the court's directives, officials who stalled, dragged their feet, wore out the litigants by a process of attrition and finally had their way by default. The court's ruling in the Marion County case was, to all practical intent, nullified by the Marion County Board.

The untimely death of Jesse K. Lewis, militant counsel for the plaintiffs, was a factor. Also the death of Mr. Rawlings, the principal plaintiff. Protestants living in the Bradfordsville area began to get discouraged and give up as the board continued its stalling tactics year after year. Eventually most of them moved away. Probably Bradfordsville today could not muster the 100 students needed for an accredited high school even if its school were to be reopened. After Jesse Lewis had obtained a new order from the Court of Appeals shortly before his death, the Marion County Board did announce that it would build a central school and ordered a bond election to finance it. Catholic Action organized and achieved the defeat of the bonds and nothing has been done since. The captive situations continue in Marion County very much as before. Most of the objectors have moved away. Those who remain are too tired to fight. The court order is still there but apparently it will never be obeyed.

One of the most recent of the "captive school" cases in which Americans United participated was the Mercer County,

Ohio case *Moore v. Board of Education.* Tried in the Court of
Common Pleas at Fort Recovery, Ohio in the spring of 1965,
the decision was handed down by Judge Frederick B. Cramer on
October 18 of that year. It was a complete triumph for the
plaintiff, Jesse C. Moore, supported by Americans United.

The complaint which had been carefully prepared by attorney Perry G. Wise charged a virtual sectarian takeover of the
public schools of Mercer County. The decision of Judge Cramer
fully supported the contention. The judge found that there existed
between the county's public school board and the Roman Catholic Church "a holy alliance" and that the arrangements between
them must be terminated.[20] He found that sectarian gerrymander-
ing of the school districts was such that while all pupils lived
in the same general area, all children attending three of the
county's schools were Catholic, while most in attendance at the
remaining school were Protestant. He pointed out that there
were even "Catholic" and "Protestant" bus routes.

Judge Cramer agreed with the plaintiff that the school board
uses "compulsory school machinery" to provide for the religious
instruction of pupils and that the board "indirectly provides the
locations suitable for and conducive to and the personnel needed
in the religious instruction . . ."[21]

The question as to whether the "captive schools" were
public or church operations intrigued Judge Cramer. He said
that it reminded him of the magician's, "Now you see it—now
you don't." "It is our opinion," he stated, "that the religious
education of the pupils attending (these schools) provided
through the 'released time' program . . . is patently woven into
the working scheme of the school and presents powerful elements
of inherent pressure by the school system in the interest of a
religious sect."[22]

The decision held that the United States Supreme Court in
the *Engel* and *Schempp-Murray* cases had "struck down, as a
violation of the 'Establishment Clause' of the First Amendment
state action considerably more feeble than that which confronts
us in the case at Bar." The conclusion of the judge was that
the program in the Mercer County schools "is founded upon a
use of the State's power of coercion which . . . determines its
unconstitutionality" and that the public schools are used as
"instruments for securing attendance at denominational classes."
He held that "the plaintiff will, therefore, be awarded that
declaratory judgment and granted such injunctive relief against
the defendant which the opinion permits and supports. . . . We
must conclude that the defendant has breached the Wall. It
must be repaired."[23]

The case of *Swart v. South Burlington (Vermont) School District* has proved to be one of the most significant ever supported by Americans United.[24] The facts of the suit were important because they offered an exact counterpart to the program of "tuition grants for parents" long advanced by Father Virgil C. Blum, S.J., and Citizens for Educational Freedom. South Burlington did not maintain a high school. Its students attended high school in other districts and, since there was no facility in their own district, a "tuition grant" was provided for their schooling. Instead of going to public schools some of the students enrolled in religious schools and drew their grants just the same. A complaint was filed on the ground that such institutions were private and thus ineligible to receive public funds and also that they were sectarian institutions forbidden to use such funds under the First and Fourteenth Amendments to the Federal Constitution.

In the winter of 1955 Glenn Archer visited Burlington, Vermont in response to appeals from local citizens and the strategy of the Vermont tuition case was planned. The first case concerned the payment of the state's share of the grants. The POAU position was sustained by the Vermont Supreme Court in October of 1956. But local boards continued to provide their share of the payments for tuition in religious schools, a practice they had been carrying on since 1880. A South Burlington citizen and taxpayer, C. Raymond Swart, was determined to press this case and sought the assistance of Americans United. Local counsel for the plaintiff was F. Ray Keyser, Jr., soon to become Governor of Vermont, and a law partner of Vermont's former Governor Stanley C. Wilson.

The suit was an important one for a second reason. It had to be based partly on the First and Fourteenth Amendments since the language of the Vermont Constitution in regard to church and state is not so specific as in many other constitutions. The Swart suit was hotly contested since, if successful, it would substantially reduce the local revenues of some of the largest Roman Catholic high schools in Vermont. The issue as to whether any public funds could be used in such fashion for indirect assistance to religious schools loomed large in the case. In most lawsuits supported by the organization Americans United made it a policy to provide only a part of the necessary funds with the rest to be raised locally. In the Swart case, however, Americans United paid all the bills.

The decision of Judge William C. Hill in the Chittenden County Court was for the plaintiff. Judge Hill held that:

As public money is being paid to a sectarian school wherein a religion is being taught, such payment violates the first command of the Everson case wherein it is stated that no contribution or tax-raised funds may be made to the support of an institution which teaches the tenets and faith of any church.[25]

The judge took particular note of the fact that courses in religion were compulsory in Burlington Catholic high schools and that these institutions were integral parts of the Roman Catholic Church. The case was promptly appealed by the South Burlington officials, supported by the Catholic diocese of Burlington. The Vermont Supreme Court completely sustained Judge Hill as it pronounced one of the most important decisions sustaining separation of church and state in many years. The Jesuit organ *America* described the decision as "alarming" and part of a scheme to impose a "secularist straitjacket on education."[26]

The South Burlington board had pleaded that it was not assisting the schools involved, only the parents who were required by law to send their children to school and had no nearby public school available. Basing its finding on the United States Supreme Court's decision in *Everson*, the Vermont Court held that the grants were tuition payments and not scholarships or awards of merit. The opinion written by Justice James S. Holden concluded:

Considerations of equity and fairness have exerted a strong appeal to temper the severity of the mandate. The price it demands frequently imposes heavy burdens on the faithful parent. He shares the expense of maintaining the public school system, yet in loyalty to his child and his belief seeks religious training for the child elsewhere. But the same fundamental law which protects the liberty of a parent to reject the public system in the interests of his child's spiritual welfare, enjoins the state from participating in the religious education he has selected.[27]

The defendants sought to take their case to the United States Supreme Court, retaining Paul Butler, former chairman of the Democratic National Committee, as their counsel. The High Court refused a review in the case thereby upholding the Vermont Court.

Yet another case of more than passing interest was one in which Americans United was not involved but for which it was directly responsible. This was the suit brought by the Christian Brothers Wineries (De La Salle Institute) to recover $490,000 in back taxes which the order claimed was unlawfully collected by the government. The Christian Brothers claimed to be a church under the definition of the regulations and therefore not liable for corporate profits tax.

The chances are that the Christian Brothers would never have been bothered by the Treasury Department had it not been for Americans United. We were advised via an embittered competitor that Christian Brothers, the largest manufacturers of commercial brandy in the United States, was not paying any tax on its profits. This was obviously unfair to other distillers who had to compete with them commercially but did have to pay their taxes. In two hearings, one in the Treasury Department and another in Congress, Americans United raised the whole issue of the profits tax exemption for churches engaged in commercial businesses. At a hearing before a House Subcommittee on Internal Revenue Taxation, November 19, 1956, Paul Blanshard, special counsel of Americans United, dramatically produced two bottles of the Christian Brothers' brandy and wine and inquired whether their production was really church business. He asserted that "to bring such activity under a clerical tax exemption umbrella simply because it is supervised by a religious order is to make a mockery of the whole concept of the function of religious institutions in our society."[28]

The Christian Brothers were frightened at the widespread publicity the disclosures had received and in 1957 began paying their taxes. Then, having protected themselves, they quietly filed suit to get their money back ($490,000) on the ground that they had been illegally taxed. The government, prodded by the enormous public interest in the case, promptly countersued for all back taxes. The case, No. 7499 in the United States District Court for the Northern District of California, Northern Division, with the De La Salle Institute as plaintiff and the United States Government as defendant would probably never have occurred had not Americans United relentlessly publicized the matter. We never received as much mail about any litigation as we did in regard to this one. The case was intriguing in that it revealed how handsome the profits were for the Brothers. In three years alone,—1952, 1953 and 1956—net profits were $3,250,000. This was, of course, only a part of the story, for the figure did not include the years 1957-1960, years in which the Brothers had expanded greatly with a slick national advertising campaign. The total must have been well beyond $7 million in net profits. Such figures had all the more interest since the Roman Catholic Church, under papal rulings, never discloses its financial status.

Christian Brothers pleaded that "plaintiff is exempt as a church." The order argued that it had chapel services at its wineries and that all its property is "subject to the control of the Pope." Judge Sherrill Halbert did not see it that way. He held that the order was not a church under the law and that it must pay up all back taxes which were due as the government alleged. This was a total of nearly $4 million. Americans United promptly raised a cry for the rewriting of Section 511 of the

Internal Revenue Code in such a manner as to eliminate from exemptions all churches or their subsidiaries engaged in competitive commercial activity.[29]

The cry was needed for the regulations were seriously at fault as Judge Halbert declared in his opinion. He ruled that the Brothers were not "sacerdotal" under the regulations, then went on to attack the regulations themselves as "invalid" and contrary to the will of Congress. The ruling held, in effect, that religious distillers should be equally vulnerable to profits tax levy with lay distillers, regardless of whether they claim to be a church, in all aspects of their unrelated business activity. "It would be impractical," he said, "to accord an exemption to every corporation which asserted itself to be a church. Obviously Congress did not intend to do this . . . If the doctrine of the Catholic Church were such, work in a winery might be a church function. . . ."[30] Stressing that the nature of the function itself must be a criterion for exemption as well as the technicalities of organization, Judge Halbert said: "This, however, could not transform an incorporated winery into an exempt church, under any reasonable interpretation of the statute . . . plaintiff is not a church."[31]

Glenn Archer did appeal to the Internal Revenue Service to change the regulation which Judge Halbert described as "invalid" and to write a new regulation consistent with his decision. He pointed out that many "unrelated businesses" of churches would continue to be exempt if their managers would qualify as "sacerdotal." Archer stated that "a new regulation would immediately affect the commercial TV-radio profits of the Jesuits, particularly in New Orleans where the order had been securing a discriminatory tax advantage over its competitors." It would also affect other church distillers and many kinds of church commercial operations. (Judge Halbert had specifically criticized tax exemption rulings favoring Loyola University in an earlier case in which Americans United filed a brief amicus curiae). Archer expressed the hope that the Christian Brothers would appeal the case so that the issue might receive the attention of the High Court. The Order never did appeal, possibly as a result of pressure from other Catholic orders which feared that such a determination might deprive them, also, of their exemption.

The Treasury Department did exactly nothing. Despite the language of Judge Halbert's opinion, despite the manifest public interest in the issue, the Department did not change or clarify the offensive regulation. Churches of various denominations are going into commercial business on an ever widening scale. Commercial operators are luring church bodies with the promise of easy money on lease-back deals which profit at the point of tax savings. This matter constitutes a growing scandal in American life and works to the discredit of the church.

Perhaps the Christian Brothers case was as important in the issue it sought to adjudicate as the Kansas City lawsuit, *Allendoerfer v. Human Resources*, which Americans United agreed to support in June, 1965. In this suit the organization challenged constitutionality of the use of federal and local funds for the support of programs carried on in religious schools. This suit brought by attorney Walter A. Raymond with the assistance of Franklin C. Salisbury, general counsel of Americans United, was designed to test government subsidies to religious institutions for welfare and educational programs. These able attorneys have succeeded Col. Edward P. Felker who gave distinguished service to Americans United as its general counsel from 1959 to 1963. The suit had such far-reaching ramifications that the United States Government at once moved to intervene.

Also working its way toward a climax in the United States Supreme Court was a case, *Horace Mann v. Tawes,* now in the Maryland Court. This suit in which Americans United has substantially assisted challenges the constitutionality under the Maryland and United States Constitutions of public grants for construction purposes to four religious institutions, Hood College, Western Maryland College, Mount St. Joseph's College and Notre Dame College of Maryland. The real objective of the suit was the vast grants for construction at religious colleges being made under the Higher Education Facilities Act of 1963.

As this was written Americans United was supporting thirteen litigations seeking to adjudicate church-state issues. The courts were apparently to be a decisive line of defense for separation of church and state in the United States.

[1] *Antonito Ledger News,* August 23, 1962.

[2] *Denver Post,* April 2, 1961.

[3] "Annual Report of the National Catholic Welfare Conference," 1961, page 29.

[4] *Zellers v. Huff,* 236 P. 2d 949 (1951), 613.

[5] *Church and State,* April, 1949.

[6] October, 1951 *Church and State: Zellers v. Huff,* 236 P. 2d 949 (1951) 613.

[7] Ibid.

[8] *Berghorn v. Franklin County School District No. 8*, Supreme Court of Missouri, No. 43,258, April Session 1953.

[9] Ibid.

[10] Ibid.

[11] Ibid.

[12] Ibid.

[13] Ibid.

[14] Ibid.

[13] *Berghorn v. Franklin County School District No. 8*, Supreme Court of Missouri, No. 43,258, April Session, 1953.

[14] Ibid.

[15] *McVey vs. Hawkins*, No. 42,903, Supreme Court of Missouri, April Session, 1953.

[16] For a good account see Harold E. Fey, *Christian Century*, November 3, 1954.

[17] See the report in *Church and State*, January, 1955.

[18] See Gainer E. Bryan, "Bradfordsville—Ten Years Later," reprint from *Western Recorder*, published by Americans United.

[19] See *Rawlings v. Butler* (1956) Ky., 290 S. W. (2d) 801. Also note *Wooley, et al v. Spalding, et al* (1956 Ky.) 293 S. W. (2d) 563.
(Copious quotes from the opinion, including these, are included in *Church and State*, July 1956.)

[20] *Moore v. Board of Education*, Mercer County, Ohio, No. 15588, October 18, 1965.

[21] Ibid.

[22] Ibid.

[23] Ibid.

[24] *Swart v. South Burlington School District*, 122 Vt. 177, cert. denied 366 U.S. 925 (1961) 425.

[25] Ibid.

[26] *America*, January 21, 1961, page 490.

[27] Op. Cit.

[28] *Church and State*, December, 1956; also July-August, 1961 and October, 1961.

[29] *Church and State*, February, 1962.

[30] *De La Salle Institute v. United States*, Civil Action No. 7499 U.S. District Court for the Northern District of California, Northern Division.

[31] Ibid.

SOUR NOTE

Father Robert F. Drinan of Boston College and Glenn L. Archer, at a meeting of the National Conference of Christians and Jews, Washington, D.C., 1963.

chapter **IX** **THE NAGGERS**

In Chapter V, I referred to the nature of the Roman Catholic effort to counter Americans United. It was keyed to a systematic avoidance of any direct confrontation on the issues. If we could be shunted off or walled off in a pocket, barred from the nerve centers of influence, then our program could make no impact on the public mind. Sometimes Catholic leaders would resort to the "whine line" of a persecuted minority to gain public sympathy. Whenever we opposed Catholic ambitions Catholic leaders would set up the cry that they were being persecuted. We would be called "bigots," "know-nothings," "Ku Klux Klan," etc. Frequently we were denounced by Catholics and their ecumenical associates among the Protestants as being "anti-Catholic."

The genius of the Catholic strategy toward Americans United was not in any single one of these elements but in the whole which they composed. All of it sought to create the impression that Americans United was an irresponsible group, that sane men, sound men, men of goodwill would not associate with it. As the ecumenical movement began to develop involving Protestants and Catholics, the idea was encouraged that participation in it would be difficult for those taking a strong stand for separation of church and state.

In the growing dialogue our hard line on church-state separation was not welcome. This was especially true because we were formidable in debate and characteristically equipped with a deeper understanding and wider knowledge of the issues than many others. Of the hundreds of dialogues and panels on church-state questions in which I have participated I can recall only about a half dozen in which I shared the program with Catholic priests or laymen. They always preferred to go on with ecumenical sentimentalists who were not apt to know very much about such matters.

This avoidance was carefully studied. It was part of the strategy of snuffing us out without a hearing. If the public could be trained to think negatively in regard to us, to go into a knee-jerk rejection of our position even before it was stated, what could be more effective? Most Catholic "replies" to Americans United never dealt with the issues in controversy between us. They were, rather, endeavors to associate us with evil men, to question our motives, to warn subtly of ostracism and boycott for those who supported our cause. The Catholic leaders sought to give us an image of being somehow unreliable and untrustworthy.

It half-way worked. Even national figures were sometimes deluded. A good example was the battle between Chet Huntley and Americans United.

Chet Huntley is a TV newscaster with NBC who has attained some prominence in association with David Brinkley on a program called the Huntley-Brinkley Report. In one of its issues CHURCH AND STATE carried an item which one of our members happened to send Chet Huntley, in what connection I do not know. When Huntley received it, instead of checking, or even thinking a little, he took the built-in Catholic reaction. Perhaps it had been sent to him in protest as he had already begun to take the Catholic line on school aid—("Religious prejudice has no place when it comes to the basic question of educating our children," etc.) At any rate, when Huntley received the item from CHURCH AND STATE, a quotation from Father Richard Ginder, one of the editors of *Our Sunday Visitor*, he dashed off a typewritten card offering to bet $5 that Father Ginder never said it.

The Ginder quote was as follows:

The Catholic Church must be the biggest corporation in the U. S. We have a branch in almost every neighborhood. Our assets and real estate holdings must exceed those of Standard Oil, A.T.&T. and U. S. Steel combined. And our roster of dues-paying members must be second only to the tax rolls of the U. S. Government.[1]

To this Huntley tossed off a reply that was to give him a few gray hairs:

I trust you will pardon me, but I do think your letter reveals some anti-Catholicism. I wish you would run down the alleged statement by Father Ginder. I will bet you $5 he did not say that. And I am not a Catholic. How about aiding chil-

dren in Catholic schools and deducting the amount of money equal to the time spent on religious instruction?

Sincerely,

Chet Huntley

This statement stung us. CHURCH AND STATE was precision edited and we had impeccable documentation for everything we printed. Here was a nationally known newscaster saying, in effect, that nothing we said could be trusted.

The reply went to our member, Mrs. Frances McConnell of Pasadena, California, who asked us to take it from there. We sent a photostatic reproduction of *Our Sunday Visitor* to Huntley and advised him to pay the $5. When confronted with the proof, Huntley who makes his living by talk lapsed into silence. When neither the $5 nor any comment was forthcoming Mrs. McConnell wrote Huntley: "Never again lay an unsolicited wager with a Southern gal who was taught at her mother's knee that a gentleman always pays his card debts."

Huntley now began to stall as we pressed him for payment. "I am sorry that I cannot accept a photostat of your articles as proof of Father Ginder's statement." This was really worse than stalling; it was crawling. Of course the photo copy was not of the CHURCH AND STATE article but of the Ginder statement in *Our Sunday Visitor,* a fact well known to Huntley if he even looked at the item.

Some on the staff were for dropping the whole matter. "You can't win a fight with Chet Huntley," they advised. But I stuck to my guns, arguing that our integrity and good name were at stake. "He made that bet and we are going to make him pay it if it's the last thing we do." We kept pecking away. Our next move was to obtain an actual copy of the May 22, 1960 issue of *Our Sunday Visitor* and send it with the quotation marked by certified mail to Chet Huntley. By now we were sharing the correspondence with the president of NBC. Again Huntley crawled. He would not even acknowledge receipt of the paper but wrote an insulting letter: "I do question your veracity. Who is Father Ginder?"

To this I replied:

Dear Mr. Huntley:

Your dilemma is this: If you acknowledge you lost and pay up like a man, you will be admitting the accuracy of CHURCH AND STATE which you are determined to avoid. On the other hand, if you don't pay, you look bad. So what do you do? You try to stall, side-step, double-talk, in the hope that you will wear us out. . . . Well, you are not going to succeed.

Cordially,

C. Stanley Lowell

When we were debating about what to do next, *The Independent* took up the cudgels with a gambit we should have thought of ourselves. It carried an account of the whole affair of Huntley's welching on the $5 bet. It urged everyone interested to send to Huntley, care of NBC, 1c in cash to help him pay. If he got anything beyond the $5 *The Independent* suggested he buy a book on ethics. Huntley was swamped with the 1c cash gifts. Here is the communication he sent to each donor:

Many thanks for your contribution. It's a pity that your prejudice and sarcasm so over-matches your respect for fact. I have been forced to conclude that there is no such man as the priest which CHURCH AND STATE ostensibly quoted. At least it fails or refuses to say where he is, who he is, or where he resides. I simply refuse to pay $5 or 5c to support that kind of cheating. I am a Protestant but your penny will go to a local Catholic charity.

Sincerely,

Chet Huntley

That was about as weak as a man could get. I almost felt sorry for Huntley. Father Ginder was a prominent priest who had written for *Our Sunday Visitor* for many years. His writings were known to millions. When Huntley tried to pretend the man did not exist it began to get on the pathetic side. But like Shakespeare's Shylock we continued to press our case. The pennies rolled in to NBC. The June, 1963 CHURCH AND STATE published a full account of the entire episode with photostatic reproductions of all relevant items. Shortly thereafter Huntley threw in the towel and sent his $5. He did it with a bad grace. I am sorely tempted to print his letter here, one of the most violent we ever received. We sent the $5 to Mrs. McConnell who promptly returned it as a donation for our educational program. September 1963 CHURCH AND STATE commented: "Mrs. McConnell's faith in the reliability of CHURCH AND STATE has now been fully vindicated. The incident is closed."

But controversies over accuracy were the least of our troubles. We were not always right and had to back down a couple of times. But we maintained an over-all average of accuracy that would compare favorably with the secular press. What made us trouble was not the challenge to our facts which we were always able and pleased to meet. It was the irrelevant smear, the McCarthy-like slur, the endeavor to label us as communists or bigots or atheists with large companies of people who accepted all this as gospel without ever asking whether or not it was true. What we feared was the false image of us created by the Catholic leadership and often meekly accepted and mouthed by Protestants who simply did not know any better.

Of course the Catholic strategy worked both ways. It helped us in many quarters. When people realized what the Catholics were trying to do they would rally to the defense of Americans United. Every attack made on us by the Catholics has invariably brought in a flood of new memberships. This was compensation for the unfairness of the attacks!

At least two full length attacks on Americans United have been distributed by the Catholic leadership. The first appeared March 28, 1951, *Who's Who in the P.O.A.U.?* It was published by *Our Sunday Visitor.* In this work guilt by association enjoys its finest hour. The 160-page book starts off with a chapter of "Some Light on Past Crusades." In this it presents in lurid detail some of the most violent anti-Catholic statements that can be assembled from the annals of American history. The implication was thus conveyed that Americans United was part and parcel of all this and represented its continuation in American life. At page 137 there is a long list of what the book calls "The Kind of People Who Make Capital of Anti-Catholic Movements." No connection with Americans United is alleged. The author has simply brought in a lot of people whom he thinks are bad. The idea seems to be that since he has put these bad people in a book with Americans United people that proves the one is just as bad as the other.

Then the author takes people he does not like and gives a chapter treatment to them—not as bad people but as people he considers wrong. For example, he has a chapter on Dr. Willard E. Givens whom he does not like. Dr. Givens had no connection with Americans United but there he is in the book anyway. The attacks on the founders of the organization such as Oxnam, Poteat, Mackay and Newton take the now thoroughly discredited line that they are communist sympathizers. They are called "very pink." The book is filled with such statements as "Perhaps he would agree with" and then follows a bitter anti-Catholic quote picked up from any source at all. The unwary reader is led to believe that this is a statement by the principal under discussion. The intellectual level of the discussion is well illustrated by the following attack on Bishop Oxnam:

Oxnam is a former president of the Federal Council of Churches of Christ in America. He passed immediately from that presidency to the presidency of the Planned Parenthood Federation, a high-sounding name for the Birth Control movement through contraceptive devices, which has Communist backing in every country which Russia would like to have become more depopulated.[2]

A sardonic overtone, and perhaps a sign of the times, is provided at page 88 and following where the author undertakes to prove that Catholic Action is not really seeking public subsidies for its schools—only fringe benefits. (Older people will no doubt recall that stage of Catholic strategy). When one compares it with the strident demands for full subsidy today, the contrast is enlightening.

Who's Who in the P.O.A.U.? is weak. Granted that the audience for which it was designed was not too erudite, still the effort was distressingly poor. CHURCH AND STATE advertised the item in its columns. Its editors felt that a wide distribution would substantially aid its cause.

The original Catholic chorus had been to the effect that Americans United would fall ("of its own weight" was the usual expression) within a year. When nothing of the kind happened and, on the contrary, the group continued to grow and thrive, Catholic leaders began to give it a second look. *Who's Who in the P.O.A.U.?* was an effort to discredit it. A more thorough-going attempt along similar lines was *United for Separation*, a work by two young Catholic laymen, Lawrence P. Creedon and William D. Falcon. This was published by the Roman Catholic Bruce Publishing Co., in 1959. Initial funds for the project were provided by Msgr. Francis J. Lally, editor of the reactionary *Boston Pilot*. The two hatchet men announced that they had greatly benefited by the counsel of a disgruntled former employee of Americans United who had been discharged by the organization. Creedon and Falcon spent more than two years of their lives working on the project.

The book must have been one of the most tedious items ever produced and shattered all records for poor sales. As I pointed out in my review:

> *Its authors try too hard. They are so manifestly eager to win the plaudits of their bishops, so furiously concerned to defend the honor of their church. They start right in at the first page and they stay with it grimly to the end.*
>
> *These men need to relax. They might have thrown in a word about POAU's defense of the Knights of Columbus against circulation of a spurious "oath," or of POAU's support of a Catholic priest in Moundsville, W. Va. .... For the sake of "appearing fair"—or, better yet, for the sake of relieving the monotony—they should have thrown in some of this. It would have made their work more effective besides helping to keep the readers awake. But they don't and the result is monotony compounded. This is fundamentally a book by bigots for bigots.*[3]

At times the authors were downright dishonest. For example, they attributed to Americans United the position that the loyalty of all Catholic candidates for public office was suspect. That, of course, was false. What Americans United had carefully done was to indicate that a Catholic candidate should make clear what he would do when the directives of his church on a "moral issue" were in conflict with his responsibility as an official of the United States.

Largest purchaser of *United for Separation* was Glenn Archer, executive director of Americans United. He sent a copy to every member of his board. The book received no attention outside the professional Catholic press—not because it was a Catholic book but because it was not a very good book.

There have been, as already indicated, various ploys by which the Catholic leadership has sought to discredit Americans United. Philadelphia in 1965 offered a splendid example of one of them. The Philadelphia archdiocese is one of the most powerful in the nation. It wields large political influence in Pennsylvania, drives bills through the Legislature, dictates to politicians. One of the startling facets of its power is its large influence with the secular press in Philadelphia. The secular press is notorious for its prompt espousal of the Catholic line on almost any public issue.

The 1965 National Conference of Americans United was held in Philadelphia. It was a sedate, serious affair. The key address was brought by Dr. John A. Mackay, former moderator of the Presbyterian Church and president emeritus of Princeton Theological Seminary. Dr. Mackay has been called "the best known Protestant Christian in the western world," since he is well known in the Latin American countries and in Europe as well as in the States. Another address was brought by Dr. Alan F. Guttmacher of New York City, president of National Planned Parenthood. There was a legal panel of distinguished attorneys discussing questions of constitutional law. The Rev. George I. Evans, a Presbyterian minister and a former official of the Pennsylvania Council of Churches, discussed the parochial bus proposal which was being pressed by Catholic Action in the state. Every last item on the program was sound, well conceived and executed. There was not a sour note anywhere.

I was in charge of press relations. To my knowledge no representative of the *Catholic Standard and Times*, the diocesan paper, or the *Philadelphia Inquirer*, one of the principal dailies, ever came near our sessions. Yet the Catholic publication published a violent attack on us as fomenters of hate, which was immediately echoed by the *Inquirer*. Here are some samples:

They wore no hoods, but they might as well have sported such attire, for shining through the outward appearance of respectability was their deep-seated opposition to the Catholic Church and everything for which it stands. Under the cloak of alleged loyalty to American ideals, with constant devotion to the U. S. Constitution and the preservation of separation of

Church and State, they stirred a witch's brew of suspicion and religious intolerance. . . .

Normally, such a hate-mongering organization would be no more welcome here than its Ku Klux Klan counterpart, but really we are fortunate that POAU came here, because it put the spotlight on the unholy alliance between certain churchmen and organizations they control in this state and POAU. As they pretend to extend the hand of friendship for civic and religious amity and cooperation, the other hand has been extended to welcome into Pennsylvania a group that exists for and thrives upon friction, a group that wants separation of Church and State, especially when the church is the Catholic Church.[4]

The attack which went to far greater length than the above quotations is rather typical of the Catholic diocesan press. The object was not Catholics but Protestants. This was the paper's way of saying that if Protestant leaders knew what was good for them they would follow the Catholic line that Americans United was a hate group and would have nothing to do with it. Indeed, the editorial (with the parochial bus bill in mind) went on to give specific warning to the State Legislature that it must pay no attention to Americans United. The diatribe was definite ground for a lawsuit for slander and libel, but we simply could not take the time and energy from our work to indulge in this sort of thing. It is offered here only to show how Americans United gets the unfortunate image it has in certain quarters. It gets it from Catholic Actionists who smear the organization as a way of overcoming its troublesome opposition.

This is the way it works: The Catholic story came out on February 5. On February 6 the *Philadelphia Inquirer,* sometimes called "the other diocesan publication," took up the Catholic story, repeated it with liberal quotes and substantial space in its columns. Neither paper had bothered to have a reporter at the sessions which they slurred so maliciously. The *Inquirer* even refused to permit any "letter to the editor" reply as though determined to see that we would have a bad image in Philadelphia.

The immediate objective was to knock Americans United out as a factor in the controversy over bus transportation for parochial schools which was then shaping up. It half-way worked too. For it did have the effect of frightening some groups in Pennsylvania from seeking the aid of Americans United. A revealing story is told by the Rev. C. Wayne Zunkel in the *Christian Century.*[5] He related how a dialogue meeting was held between Protestant and Catholic leaders and that the former had the impression that Catholic Action would not press the bus bill in 1965. While the Protestants were basking in this belief nothing definite was heard from the Catholics on the matter. They were, however, hard at work setting up the bus drive which the Protestants were convinced they would not make.

When the story leaked out that the bill was ready to go and that Governor Scranton had even agreed to make it part of his legislative proposals, the opposition belatedly got into action. A group called Friends of the Public Schools was formed. One of its cardinal principles, according to Zunkel, was that there would be no cooperation whatsoever with Americans United. They insisted on this point because they did not want to disrupt ecumenical relations with the Catholic brethren. No one must suspect that their activity was "anti-Catholic" and any kind of association with Americans United might be so construed.

What happened? This is kind of funny. They got tagged with "bigotry" anyway! The *Catholic Standard and Times* which seldom bothers to check facts made a violent attack on the Friends of the Public Schools and termed it "a new organization formed by POAU, an anti-Catholic propagandist organization with headquarters in Washington, D.C." and referred to the Friends' chairman as "an active organizer on behalf of POAU."[6] The Friends had tried to be pure but they failed. They fought the battle like perfect gentlemen, just as the Catholic leaders had stipulated, and what did it get them? A fat defeat. Had they waged their campaign as a cooperative venture with all the help they could get, they would probably have won. In this instance the Philadelphia Catholic leadership shrewdly divided the forces against it, blackened the image of Americans United and got transportation at public expense—all in one neat operation. Who was it that said, "Nice guys finish last." The Catholics administered to Zunkel and his group the same kind of treatment they had given Americans United for years and for the same reason. Someone was in their way.

The Philadelphia archdiocese used another group in its campaign against Americans United. Most urban communities today have a Human Relations Commission by whatever name it may be called whose business is to promote good relations among racial and religious groups. In Philadelphia it is called the Fellowship Commission. It is composed of nice, but gullible, Philadelphians. The Catholics went to this group with copies of the *Catholic Standard* story and other items about Americans United and persuaded the Commission's Committee on Community Tensions that the group had used unfair tactics in the controversy over the parochial bus bill. The Americans United literature which had been distributed was to be condemned as "irrelevant, unwarranted and hate-making arguments," said its chairman Emil F. Goldhaber.

This opinion was apparently rendered entirely on the basis of the Catholic complaint. Certainly no representative of Americans United was ever invited to appear before the committee. The committee merely permitted itself to be used in a maneuver to discredit Americans United. In a delighted front-page article in the *Standard and Times*, the Catholic paper gloated over the denunciation. Then, sure enough, the faithful Catholic echo, the *Philadelphia Inquirer*, came through with the old "one-two" and they even got *Religious News Service* to make it a threesome.

This one was too good for the *Brooklyn Tablet* to resist. Along side its story in the July 15, 1965 issue on "CEF National Award to Gov. Rockefeller," the *Tablet* blazed: "City of Brotherly Love Finds POAU Guilty of Hate." That was a good one. Then the *Tablet* rehashed the *Standard* and *Inquirer* story and, for good measure, added a pious quote from Catholic Actionist William B. Ball: "The Fellowship Commission has rendered a signal service in denouncing appeals to religious bigotry which were made and are being continued on the school bus issue."

People are always asking why we have an anti-Catholic image. The answer is that the Catholics give it to us and the Protestants help them. It certainly beats having to meet our arguments.

Catholic Actionists were always trying to persuade the Jews to attack Americans United as a "hate group." In spite of the many attempts that were made, I can recall only one instance in which Catholics were successful in this. This instance was never repeated and I have reason to believe it was honestly regretted. The Jews—in this instance the Commission on Social Action of Reform Judaism—were extremely sensitive on the matter of a "religious test" for public office and made common cause with the Catholics in regard to it during the 1960 campaign. They were apparently led by some Catholic friends in New York to believe that Americans United was trying to raise a "religious test" in regard to a Catholic's candidacy for the Presidency. This was, of course, exactly the opposite of our position. But in view of our role as critic of certain Catholic political programs it might have been easy to believe that we were opposed to a Catholic for the Presidency.

Having been persuaded that this was indeed our position, without any consultation with us, and, obviously without much study of our literature on the Presidential issue, Albert Vorspan of the Commission attacked us in the press for "injecting anti-Catholic bigotry" into the 1960 campaign. It was my responsibility to straighten Mr. Vorspan out which I did in a letter of April 14, 1959:

I call your attention to a quotation in the New York Times of April 10, in which Senator Kennedy states that he regards questions regarding the effect of a candidate's religion on his conduct of civil duties as a proper matter for discussion in a political campaign. This has always been the position of POAU and Senator Kennedy has agreed with us completely. I cannot see why you should attempt to suppress this issue. If you think it should be suppressed, it is of course your right to state your position, but to question the good faith of POAU in stating our position does seem quite gratuitous. . . . I wonder if you people know who your friends are.

Other than this unfortunate episode we have always enjoyed the best relations with all sectors of the variegated Jewish community. This community, with the exception of one tiny splinter group, has presented a solid front for public support of public education and no public support for religious education.

One of the common criticisms of Americans United was especially dear to Catholic Action since it had appeal for Protestants as well. This was the line that it was a "secularist" organization, that it was driving God out of this or that and helping to produce an atheistic culture. Almost at random I draw from a sheaf of these an item from the Dayton, Ohio *Journal Herald*, March 30, 1963. It is an attack on Americans United by the Rev. Frederick A. Pope, rector of St. George's Episcopal Church. He declared that the position of Americans United was "misleading to many people. They think that our Constitution was written by atheists and thus has no undergirding in Christian principles." He complained that "groups like POAU are trying to eradicate every part of religion from the public schools. As your rector, I ask you to beware of POAU." He then added a sentence which may have revealed his real motive. He said: "POAU is not among us to reconcile but to divide." This reference was apparently to the controversy over parochial bus transportation at public expense which was already becoming an issue in Ohio. Mr. Pope's church later gave its official endorsement to this Catholic effort in the Legislature. Since POAU's opposition to any use of public funds for religious schools was well known, Mr. Pope was apparently helping to work up a consensus for it by classifying the opposition as "dividers."

The "divisive" line was also taken by Catholics. A Jesuit priest from Marquette University, Father William F. Kelley,

Oops,
Sorry!

made a bitter attack on Americans United, calling it "the most divisive factor in any cooperation of church groups today."[7] And why was the organization divisive? Because, explained Father Kelley, it was trying to block the Jesuits of Marquette University from realizing their land acquisition goals in Milwaukee through a proposed university-city-federal renewal project! The motive was not always as transparent as in this case where it was candidly admitted by the priest. But the motive was always there: "You are in our way; therefore you are bad."

A humorous depiction of the "divisive" theme can be found in a cartoon printed in the *Catholic Herald,* March 14, 1963. It shows POAU sitting in the midst of an ecumenical orchestra playing a symphony entitled "Inter-Faith Harmony." But POAU whanging away at a little old triangle is sounding a "Sour Note" and other members of the group are looking at him in anger. The moral would appear simple—everybody who stands in the way of giving the Catholic Church what it wants is sounding a sour note. All should join the ecumenical chorus and give the Catholics what they demand.

Protestant criticism of Americans United was often based on the premise that it was rude to say anything critical of a church and particularly the Roman Catholic Church. Sometimes this led to amusing denouements. The *Christian Century,* an independent journal on the liberal wing of Protestantism, had in the forties and fifties been friendly to Americans United. But with the coming of Martin Marty to the staff, a man immersed in the ecumenical movement, the journal began to change. Marty was so anxious to criticize Americans United in order to establish himself with his ecumenical friends that on at least one occasion he was badly trapped.

THE NAGGERS

In the *Christian Century* of September 18, 1963, Marty attacked Americans United. He charged us with taking up the cudgels for Rolf Hochhuth's play, "Der Stellvertreter," which criticized the role of Pope Pius XII in regard to the Nazi persecution of the Jews. The fact is that our article had never mentioned the Hochhuth play at all. It had dealt with the problem of Pius XII and the Jews but in the context of discussing the accession of Pope Paul VI who had been intimately associated with Pius XII. Marty primly assured us that we had "no competence" to discuss the matter and should be silent.

Since I had written the original article I replied to Marty by pointing out that if he had taken the trouble to consult the back files of his own publication he would find in them articles by me discussing the very issue which he was sure I had no competence to discuss.[8] I reminded him that I had been in Germany at the time, had observed the problem first-hand, and that the *Century* had thought well enough of my observations to print them. My comment: "Church-state involvements have been the bane of Italy and scarcely less so of Europe. An assessment of Pope Paul's proclivities in this area would seem to be relevant to any estimate of his reign." The reply in *Church and State* ended as follows:

It was for the purpose of providing candid and independent analysis that a journal like Church and State came into existence and its willingness to do so explains its rapid growth. It can speak in frankness where the secular press and conventional Protestant journalism now fear to tread. The Century should be glad of this.[9]

No more was heard on this point from Marty.

The Jesuit organ *America* always presented itself as an ultra-pure, high-level journal. Usually its only recognition of Americans United was a snide aside from time to time which we simply ignored. One time, though, *America* riled us. *America* liked to pretend that its high-flown verbiage put it in the stratosphere of the chaste whereas we with our direct, say-what-you-mean language were low life. In its issue of March 31, 1962, the Jesuits undertook to develop this thesis. They had been saving up some of our more direct quotes for years and now put them all on display. Their argument was that direct language like this somehow made us unfit to associate with gentlemen (like them and all decent people who, of course, took their line). This was too much. It provoked the following editorial, "Masters of Deceit," which is reproduced in full.

The Jesuits do not like our language. The Jesuit publication, America, devotes a considerable portion of its March 31 issue to pointing this out. Many examples are offered to prove the pet Jesuit contention that we are "bigots" and that, therefore, it is unnecessary to deal with our arguments.

Our language is too direct, too "unbuttoned," to use Fr. Davis' expression. It does not surprise us at all that the Jesuits should feel this way about our words. We always make the point without fooling around. In the Jesuit code this is an unforgivable sin.

When we deal with the Jesuits we are dealing with men steeped in a centuries' old tradition of deceit. We are dealing with men trained from early youth in the fine art of using words to conceal meaning rather than to convey it. We are dealing with an order that has been expelled from one country after another because its members were archconspirators whom nobody could trust.

A Jesuit never thinks in a straight line. He is trained not to. If he is going from New York to Washington, he will go by way of Rome—always. When such a man speaks he is quite incapable of a simple "Yea" or "Nay."

A good example of the Jesuit art is seen in the writing of Fr. John Courtney Murray. This Jesuit writer has made the front page of Time with an ambiguous book on Catholicism and American concepts of freedom in which he purports to show, by reinterpreting old papal utterances, that freedom might be awarded to Protestants in an ultimate Catholic America without actually violating that Church's teaching.

But Fr. Murray has never demanded freedom of thought within his own Church, never championed the cause of the oppressed Protestants in Catholic countries, nor opposed the basic denials of freedom contained in Roman Catholic Canon Law. Yet Fr. Murray's studied vagueness and superb double talk have stirred doting admiration in soft Protestant circles.

It is not hard to see why CHURCH AND STATE offends the Jesuit mind. It does not beat properly about the bush. Its language is designed not to conceal truth but to express it accurately and fairly. In CHURCH AND STATE the casuistry and double-entendre so dear to the heart of the Jesuit simply have no place.

Hence, we are a stumbling block and offense to that group. Because we and the Jesuits use language for different purposes, we do not really speak the same language. "You can tell a lot about a person," says Fr. Davis, "by the way he uses words." We agree, and the Jesuit words are, we believe, an excellent index to the Jesuit character.

Let us examine the Jesuit words and the POAU words as used to describe the same thing. Let the reader himself judge. "Independent schools" (Jesuit). "Schools wholly owned and controlled by priests of the Roman Catholic Church" (POAU). "Freedom of choice in education" (Jesuit). "Canon Law 1374 denies freedom of choice in education to Catholic parents, ordering them to send their children to Catholic schools" (POAU). "Justice for children" (Jesuit). "Subsidies for Catholic schools" (POAU).

To continue the parallel: "Complex religio-ethnic group struggle" (Jesuit). "Catholic political pressure" (POAU). Federal aid to church schools is "not a religious matter;" it is "a political question" (Jesuit). Federal aid to church schools means a "tax for religion" (POAU). "POAU—vigilantes of intolerance" (Jesuit). "POAU, defenders of the wall of church-state separation" (POAU).

Some find the Jesuit approach preferable. It is certainly more comforting for men who do not want to face issues or even, perhaps, to know what they are. We, ourselves, concede that the Jesuits outdo us in many ways. The paper in their publication is slicker than ours and that is as it should be. Their number of pages is just twice as great. That, too, is appropriate, for double talk requires twice the space of straight talk. Yet we believe there is one thing we have that the Jesuits do not have—integrity.[10]

The Jesuits subsided—for the time being.

One of the forms of sniping that went on constantly was the charge that our leaders were "communistic." The Catholics used this line in the McCarthy period when it had its vogue. They dropped it in the late 1950's but other sources kept it up. One of the persistent purveyors of this line was Edgar C. Bundy of Wheaton, Ill. We were frequently attacked in the sheet he put out called *News and Views*. His issue of March, 1962, for example, was entirely devoted to a smear attack on us. Some idea of the quality of the material can be seen from the following paragraph:

Not only were a rather large number of (POAU) founders and officers individuals with Communist front records, but the urgency for its creation in 1947 just happened to coincide with Soviet Russia's resumption of unlimited political warfare against the United States. This may have been purely an unfortunate coincidence—on the other hand it may not have been.[11]

The smear material followed the usual line of these "communist" attacks. It purported to show that officials of Americans United had been members of groups which had in them some bad people, even some communists. This proved that they, too, were bad and communist. In a letter to reply to its inquiring members regarding this kind of attack Americans United offered specific answers on behalf of its officials, then commented:

Of course our leaders are articulate men. They have spoken; they have associated with others in common ventures. They have their opinions and they express them. They are not jellyfish. The men who seek to assassinate their characters are men who have their own axes to grind. They are men who made a handsome living out of others under a charge of "communism"... This kind of human carrion has itself become suspect of late. These are the men who divide the country, the men who pit neighbor against neighbor in a welter of mutual suspicion and fear.... It is time for somebody to have the courage to stand up and tell them off once and for all.

How Protestants should ignore Americans United and even put it out of existence was explained in a little lecture to them volunteered by Father Albert C. Kolch of the Detroit archdiocese in that group's official publication, the *Detroit World*. He started off with the tattered Catholic line:

POAU is the ideological successor of the "know nothings," American Protective Association, and Ku Klux Klan.... At a time when prejudice is very unpopular in America the organization hides behind the more popular "separation of church and state" label.

Then Father Kolch made a simple request of Protestants: "All I ask," he said, "is that non-Catholics of good will ignore POAU and give us the same fair treatment."

When the Methodist General Conference of 1960 endorsed Americans United after a four-year study by its Coordinating Council, Roman Catholic Bishop Robert Dwyer gave the body a disapproving lecture in the Los Angeles *Catholic Tidings* of July 1, 1960. He urged Methodists to reverse their position since they had, he said, by this action endorsed "that body dedicated to secularist divisiveness."

America, the Jesuit publication, suggested that the Methodists had done a shameful thing in this endorsement since "POAU has acquired an unenviable reputation as the heir to a long line of bigoted anti-Catholic organizations that have disgraced the history of this democracy. The Denver vote by the official representatives of 9.6 million Methodists, was in itself a grim index of the survival of anti-Catholic feeling and a setback to Catholic-Protestant dialogue."[12] This was an open invitation to the ecumenical crowd to get busy.

While we had to struggle along under a burden of disapproval from the Catholic clergy, this was not always the case with the laity of that church. Many of our Protestant critics have found it difficult to believe that we have had from the very first a considerable contingent of Catholic members. Some of these, to be sure, are mere curiosity seekers who are eager to learn what we are going to do next. But many are bonafide members who gleefully applaud whenever we tangle with the officialdom of their church. The fact is that there are millions of Catholics in the United States who have never given more than a passing nod to the clerical direction of their lives which is such a manifest part of Roman Catholic policy. They practice birth control right along, insisting that this is none of the church's business. They send their children to public schools in spite of the official rule. They evidence every disposition to think for themselves. Vatican Council II has enormously stimulated such a development within the Roman Catholic communion.

These hardy souls, at least a goodly number of them, have always belonged to Americans United. They believe in the separation of church and state. Indeed, they really believe in it for they are generally well aware of what union of church and state has done to their church in certain historic situations. Sometimes our Catholic members misunderstand our role. They think of us as a kind of policeman of the churches. They want us to "clean up" certain things in the Catholic Church of which they disapprove. This, of course, is none of our business. So long as no law is violated, the internal management of churches is not our concern. I could supply a number of humorous instances of those who encouraged us to do otherwise.

Among Protestants our fiercest enemies were of two kinds: those whose toes we had stepped on in some church-state controversy and denominational leaders of the particular agency which handled church-state matters. Consider the latter. In certain instances we were estranged from denominational boardsmen by their sensitivity to professional prerogative. It was distressing to learn that the very leaders whose concerns coincided generally with our own could be our most violent foes.

Fortunately, this was not always true. Our counterparts in the National Association of Evangelicals and the Seventh-day Adventists, for example, were uniformly friendly. We did not always agree with each other but maintained amicable and cooperative relations at all times.

With the old-line Protestant boardsmen, however, the story was sometimes different. These men often disliked us because they felt that we stood in their way. Some of them even said so. After all, had they not been appointed by their denomination to handle church-state matters? Ought not their co-religionists to be looking to them for direction in this field? Whence, then, these interlopers? Their people should be looking to "responsible leaders" (themselves) for guidance and not to "outsiders."

The cogency of our program was such that when we were able to reach the people in the pews, and in the local boards and councils and associations of the churches, we were invariably well received. Sometimes the disgruntled professionals of the denomination would seek to thwart us at this point and even to divert support from us. At times they were in the embarrassing position of fighting us even when positions on a particular issue might be identical.

There has been an unfortunate deterioration in the position of some of the Protestant leaders on these issues. Some of them simply do not believe in church-state separation. The liberal leadership of Protestantism has in certain instances struck a church-state agreement with the Roman Catholic leadership through the ecumenical movement. This leadership can no longer be trusted by those who believe in a strict separation of church and state. It is time to state candidly that the rank and file membership of the old-line Protestant denominations which does continue to uphold church-state separation will find its consistent champion in Americans United. The rank and file should begin to speak to its own leadership which has been sadly misleading it.

The personal pique of a prominent Methodist layman, Robert B. Pease of Pittsburgh, resulted in his violent attack on us at the Methodist General Conference in that city in 1964. The Pease attack was assisted by professional leaders of the Methodist Board of Social Concerns. Back of the Pease vendetta against Americans United lay a long story involving urban redevelopment. Robert Pease was head of Urban Redevelopment programs in Pittsburgh. He was the administrator responsible for agreeing to use of eminent domain to acquire on Pittsburgh's bluff a 34-acre tract for the Holy Ghost Fathers, a Roman Catholic order which operates Duquesne University. The program would cost $9.2 million in public funds, according to the first report of the project and would oust 445 families from their homes and 135 businesses.

While there were many such programs going on throughout the country for the benefit of churches, this one appeared to be particularly objectionable. This was so because of the large number of homes and businesses to be destroyed and, even more, because the area was not really blighted. It was, in fact, a better-than-average neighborhood with substantial homes of middle class and sound small businesses. The protests of the victims were vehement. There were many appeals to Americans United, some of them from Catholic residents of the area. In reaction to the outburst of public anger and the systematic protests of Americans United and other groups, the project was eventually trimmed to 22 acres, but the cost to the government had meanwhile risen to $10,745,915. The "resale" price to Duquesne was announced as $954,000. The Holy Ghost Fathers, who thus acquired a large site of extremely valuable land at a bargain price from the government, then proposed to erect their buildings with funds obtained from the government under the Higher Education Facilities Act.

We would have supported Catholic plaintiffs in a lawsuit, but we had already been beaten in a number of challenges to urban renewal procedures in church-state situations. There was no reason to believe we could succeed in Pittsburgh. But one thing we could do was to educate the public as to what was going on and that we did with steady persistence. Robert Pease, who with Father Henry J. McAnulty, president of Duquesne, had arranged the operation, was incensed at the opposition of Americans United. He felt that the group was interfering with work he was trying to do for the good of Pittsburgh.

There was another redevelopment deal in the Pittsburgh area which aroused public opinion. This was not the immediate responsibility of Robert Pease since it lay beyond the boundaries of Pittsburgh in Allegheny County, but it did stir fresh criticism of the Greater Pittsburgh redevelopment program. The large school of St. Coleman's Roman Catholic parish in Turtle Creek, a suburb of Pittsburgh, was so unfortunate as to have located immediately next door, almost under its eaves, the Free Gospel Church, a small, frame structure. St. Coleman's had long coveted the property of the Free Gospel Church and its offers to buy had become so frequent as to amount almost to harassment. The Rev. George M. Baker, pastor of the Free Gospel Church, did not want to sell. He and his congregation were happy where they were.

Finally St. Coleman's leaders had the bright thought of using an urban redevelopment program with the government's power of eminent domain to oust the Free Gospelers and get their land. This plot was exposed by *Church and State* and a build up of public opinion against the program began in Pittsburgh. This program was, in fact, upset as a result of a public hearing finally achieved through popular demand. Attorney Charles C. Arensberg, Jr., assisting the Free Gospel Church at the request of Americans United, stated at the hearing: "This is the first time in the history of urban redevelopment in Pennsylvania that anyone has proposed taking the property of one church for the benefit of another."[13] Alarmed at the tide of public opinion, Auxiliary Bishop Vincent M. Leonard, representing the Pittsburgh diocese, announced that St. Coleman's would not take the Protestant property after all.

These and other redevelopment deals in the Pittsburgh area had brought Americans United into frequent combat with Robert Pease. He apparently was determined to get the organization and with the coming of the Methodist General Conference to Pittsburgh in the spring of 1964 he saw his opportunity. Pease was elected one of the lay delegates from the Pittsburgh area and thus had access to the Conference floor. He was also, in effect, the Conference host, which placed him in an advantageous position. On the final day of the Methodist General Conference of 1964, Robert Pease took the floor under a point of personal privilege. He made a violent and irresponsible attack on Americans United to the accompaniment of carefully rehearsed headlines in the Pittsburgh papers. He charged that Americans United had distributed false and salacious literature and that the organization had attacked his integrity as a public official. He had, in short, been treated disgracefully and could hold his peace no longer.

Mr. Pease was heard with respect by the Conference. His posture of outraged purity impressed the majority who had no understanding of the real issues in the case. But Mr. Pease was a prejudiced witness. He made his living in urban redevelopment. We had criticized the urban redevelopment procedures which he directed. He was given the floor of the General Conference to air charges against his critics. Amazingly and incredibly, Methodist ministers on the staff of Americans United, sitting in the audience, were denied any opportunity to reply. That this could have happened in the highest responsible body of a church which prizes itself on its fairness and democracy is simply beyond belief. It did happen, nevertheless.

The Pease vendetta cost Americans United its traditional endorsement by the Methodist Church. We were not unaware of our danger when we undertook to challenge this prominent Methodist in the Pittsburgh controversy. If we had it to do over again, though, we would follow the same course. Our members have come to expect from us this kind of direct intervention in the most controversial of issues. We have tried to do our job and left the caution to others.

Church and State ruminated on the incident:

One good thing should come from this delegate's unfair and unwise attack on POAU. It should lay to rest his canard (and that of others) that we are an anti-Catholic organization. The attack neatly points up the fact that we are just as anti-Methodist as we are anti-Catholic when a Methodist or a Catholic is wrong on church-state.[14]

A comparable though minor episode took place in June, 1965 at the meeting of the Baltimore Annual Methodist Conference. At this session the Rev. John R. Bucheister, pastor in Westminster, Maryland, took the floor to attack Americans United and to ask deletion from its budget of a $500 annual allocation to the legal activities of the organization. He offered many pretexts for his behavior but never gave the real reason— namely that he wanted to punish us for our supporting a lawsuit in the Court of Maryland challenging a public grant of $500,000 for construction on the campus of Western Maryland College, a Methodist institution located in Mr. Bucheister's town of Westminster, Maryland.

After this one we felt like repeating our September, 1964 editorial.

The sum total of the attacks made upon us from so many quarters was to convince us that we could never be very popular and that even the slickest public relations people would probably be unable to create a "good image" for us. New members would come to the staff (I was one of them) with the blithe assumption that if we just trimmed a bit here and if we were a bit more cautious there we could gain acceptance and popularity. Outsiders are always telling us: "You fellows have an important and useful operation but you run it in the wrong way and get everybody down on you." Well, we are not immune to errors and we have made some. But the point is that the very nature of our operations is such as to make important people angry with us. These are important people in the leadership of the churches. These are important people in government. After all you cannot go about the business of depriving church officials of many millions of dollars in public funds which they believe are due them and expect them to like you. You cannot mess up the best-laid plans of government officials for programs in conjunction with church leaders and expect them to like you. The best you can hope for is grudging approval of those who admire you for doing something that everybody else is afraid to do, yet regret that it has to be done.

Why do it? Why take this incessant flow of abuse from all quarters? Surely there are easier ways to make a living. Yes, there are. The reason Glenn Archer took on the work of Americans United I tried to explain in Chapter II. He is an exemplar of a vanishing breed—the reformer. Every person who has ever come to the staff of Americans United and stayed with it is one also. He would have to be. These are people who are piloted by the preposterous notion that God has called them to do a job in this world and they had better do it. There is in these staff men the zeal of the reformer, the guts of the crusader, the drive of the missionary who faces obviously hopeless odds because God expects it of him.

To maintain an effective separation of church and state—for the good of both—in the United States is the passion of Americans United. This is the meat and drink of its staff members. It is written across their brains and hearts. To assume that they will be discouraged or worn out by abuse and betrayal is to reason as the Gentiles. That is not going to happen. It was once said of another group but without due strain it could also be said of the staff of Americans United:

Neither snow nor rain, nor heat, nor gloom of night stays these couriers from the swift completion of their appointed rounds.

[1] *Our Sunday Visitor*, Vol. XLIX—No. 4, May 22, 1960 (It's really there).

[2] *Who's Who in the POAU?* page 28.

[3] *Church and State*, January, 1960.

[4] *Catholic Standard and Times*, February 5, 1965 and *Philadelphia Inquirer*, February 6, 1965.

[5] *Christian Century*, August 25, 1965.

[6] *Catholic Standard and Times*, January 29, 1965.

[7] *Milwaukee Journal*, May 1, 1963.

[8] *Church and State*, November, 1963.

[9] *Church and State*, November, 1963.

[10] *Church and State*, June, 1962.

[11] *News and Views* published by Editor Edgar C. Bundy, March, 1962.

[12] *America*, May 28, 1960.

[13] *Church and State*, January, 1965.

[14] *Church and State*, September, 1964.

Hope
Chest

Associate Director
C. Stanley Lowell,
testifying at a
congressional hearing
June 6, 1961.

chapter **X** **MAKING A MARK**

How to be heard from, how to make some mark on the life and thought of the nation in terms of the organization's avowed purpose—this was the problem that confronted Glenn Archer when he assumed direction of Americans United. The first thing he had to do was to raise some money. There was no budget and no observable source of income to support it if there were one. It is a favorite stance of foundation supported or denomination-supported agencies to look down on Americans United because "that outfit has to raise money." They seem to assume that because they can sit comfortably with their salaries and expenses guaranteed, this renders them holy men, unsullied by the toil and moil.

Now strange as it may seem such men are not apt to drive very hard for their cause. Whatever is assured is not characteristically capable of drive. The sure income induces complacency. Being devout separationists we would quickly seize upon this observation as an analogy for church-state separation. Theoretically, the kept church can do the job much better than one scrounging for its support. The money issue is out of the picture and the leaders can concentrate on the job their church has to do. In practice, however, it does not seem to work that way. Let government establish a church—build it, heat it, provide it with an eloquent preacher and sound music—and what do you have? A built-in formula guaranteed to produce sterility. But let there be a tiny, struggling congregation, straining to pay its clergy and provide a suitable place of worship, and here you are apt to find the real dynamic of religion in a company of faithful who are really faithful.

Why has Americans United consistently demonstrated that its output and activity are greater despite the fact that it must raise its own budget, than is the case with comparable groups that have assured sources of income? The explanation may lie in this area now under exploration. At any rate, we challenge any comparable group in the United States to match the extent and variety of our activities during the past 19 years. We have done all this—and raised our budget too. If this sounds like a reminder of the organization's financial needs, that is what it is.

How to move—how to educate—how to reach the people— this was the basic Archer problem. The founders had lent their names to the project. They were some of the biggest names in education and among the Protestant clergy in the United States. This was a help. But the owners of those names could offer little direct assistance. They had duties of their own. Aside from coming to the annual meeting and lending words of encouragement, there could be no direct assistance from this quarter.

In the early days Glenn Archer formed a lasting association with the Scottish Rite Masons of the Southern Jurisdiction, which proved most helpful. Funds for the first building which the organization purchased on Massachusetts Avenue in Washington, were provided by its Supreme Council at the time when John H. Cowles was Sovereign Grand Commander. Under the succeeding Commanders, Thomas J. Harkins and Judge Luther A. Smith, this fine relationship has continued. These men were all no-nonsense Americans. They believed in the public schools and in the separation of church and state. They quickly saw in the director of Americans United a man who could be trusted to support actively the ideals of Americanism which were dear to them. He was a man worthy of support.

One of Archer's problems was that outside of his native Kansas he was unknown. People could not support what they did not know. He set out to correct this. He formed a policy of accepting every single invitation to speak that he could possibly make. It mattered not how big the crowd. He was not proud; he would go. He went everywhere, riding a bus as long as 36 hours to arrive. Being a captivating speaker, an art he astutely cultivated, he began to be known as "a good man" for a convention or church program. Soon his invitations began to multiply and became, as they are to this day, far more than he can handle. He took all that two or three men possibly could and everywhere he went he preached the gospel of church-state separation and of Americans United, the guardian of the wall. He began to get support. People were impressed with the sincerity of this rugged man from Kansas. They believed in him;

they believed in what he was trying to do for the country and for the churches. Financial support flows after such belief.

For years Archer would have no budget of proposed expenses and anticipated income. Since he had no assured source of income and had to operate on the basis of "what came in," why should he bother to put a budget on paper? He argued that he would operate on the funds that he was able to raise, whatever those turned out to be. But after the early years, as a certain sturdiness of financial support was achieved, it became possible to predicate a budget together with at least general sources of anticipated income. From the very start there was no hocus pocus about finances at Americans United. Everybody who touched money was bonded. The financial affairs were carefully audited by an outstanding firm of accountants. Archer never delegated financial responsibility. He followed these matters personally every day. The annual audit was always ready for the board when it assembled for the annual meeting. In all the 19 years there has never been a nickel unaccounted for or the slightest suspicion of irregularity. That is the way Archer works. He had dealt with money all his life and knew how to use it and save it. People contributed to Americans United because they liked the cleanness of the financial operation. They knew that their money would go for the cause they wanted to support. A few knew that Archer was personally paying many of the expenses.

Nobody was permitted to make anything that whispered of a racket out of Americans United. If any of us on the staff were invited to speak or preach or write, whether it bore any relation to the program of Americans United or not, he was required to turn in his honorarium to the corporation. Even ministers speaking on a Sabbath during "off" hours turned their honoraria over to the corporation. No speaker would neglect the small church for the large. We got one salary in the service of a cause that demanded our full time and attention, and everything that we produced went to that cause. Archer made the rule and followed it religiously himself. All the rest of us did, too. Most of the financial support for Americans United—80 per cent at least—has always come from individual donors. Most of these gifts are in small amounts.

There was the problem of organization—an insoluble problem for a group like Americans United. At first, part of the board believed that local organizations of Americans United would not be needed. Many of them were churchmen. They thought of the organization as spreading its message through the churches and their various groups. Some were educators and lawyers. They thought of Americans United as reaching into the professional organizations and publications. Would separate groups at the local or state level be necessary? They inclined to think not. Why not operate through existing groups and save the trouble and expense?

Americans United has always related itself usefully to existing groups. For years it has had a Department of Church Relations headed by Herbert S. Southgate, a Methodist minister. Associated with him is Gioele Settembrini, a Baptist minister. There are more than 1,000 "scroll churches" in the United States which make a provision for Americans United in their annual budgets and receive a bundle of *Church and State* for their distribution among official members. Every year speakers from the staff fill literally hundreds of engagements for churches and their related organizations. Most Protestant colleges and seminaries have been visited by representatives of Americans United in a continuing program of campus activity. All such programs are now part of the basic operation. Less significant, but always a part of the program, has been the reach to educational and legal groups, to service clubs, PTA's and the like.

Yet, Archer soon began to see that some kind of structure across the nation was necessary if the organization were to assume significant stature and influence. John C. Mayne of Missouri was the first director of organization. He was succeeded by Edward Terry of Portland, Oregon, and later by Gaston D. Cogdell of Cincinnati who serves in the post today.

The organization and administration of locals constituted perhaps the most serious problem confronting the leadership of Americans United. To begin with they were volunteer groups. Nobody got paid for anything. In fact, the officers were often tagged for some of the expenses themselves. They had to be devoted people, clearly, or they would not have taken on such a job. Sometimes the problem was that the able people who could have been effective did not want to be bothered and the ineffective people were the ones who offered. Often we have been criticized because our local leadership was not appealing. Yet these very people were the ones who began to build our movement into a power. Maybe they did not do things just right but they did them. They were heard from; their community knew they were there. We are everlastingly indebted to our local leaders.

It should certainly be added that we had some very brilliant and competent leaders of our local chapters. I think of men like Victor B. Harris and Ralph Neuhoff, St. Louis attorneys, who made our chapter there a powerful educational and legal force in Missouri. They were exceedingly able men who gave many hours of their high-priced time to the work of Americans United. Although both have now died there are others who share their vision and their determination to maintain the effort for church-state separation.

Though many laymen of the churches, and even some of no formal religious faith, hold posts of local leadership, it is the clergy who have in so many instances served as our leaders and borne the brunt of the attacks which sometimes came. This book contains some criticisms of the old line Protestant leadership. Let it be said here that Americans United could not have achieved anything were it not for its friends among this same leadership. Among the Protestant pastors are men of rare courage who will indeed put their necks out for a worthy cause even though that cause is not always popular. This refers not only to the prominent Protestant churchmen who founded Americans United in the first place, but also to a host of lesser known ministers who have opened their churches, served on the boards, defended and promoted from dawn till dusk. Without them we would be nothing.

It was soon discovered that what would bring a local into existence and keep it going was a local controversy. Only our larger chapters with solid leadership appeared able to sustain themselves through the years without faltering. If there were a local church-state controversy and we were called in to advise or arbitrate, this tended to result in the formation of a chapter. If we agreed to support a lawsuit in the community, this would solidify the organization. So long as the matter was in litigation our chapter grew and thrived. Once the issue had been resolved, however, the local tended to go into decline. This was human and understandable, but it gave organization the headache of impermanence.

The money problem with locals was always with us. The minute a local came into existence it might want to use all the funds produced in that community for local operations. In such a situation the national organization would be worse off than if there were no local at all. Yet, one way or another we had to have locals. We tried first one formula, then another, and what obtains now is the result of a long agony of experience. Nothing is surer, however, than that it will prove unsatisfactory and have to be abandoned in favor of something different. Nevertheless, through this kind of struggle, in spite of occasional betrayal and subversion by local leaders, amid maledictions and perfidy, Americans United has slowly and painfully built its structure across the nation.

In 1949 in his report to the Washington, D. C. area membership of Americans United at Constitution Hall, Glenn Archer announced certain organization goals:

In order to achieve our objective and fulfill our mission, we propose to launch a campaign to raise one million dollars . . . to enlighten and mobilize public opinion in support of religious liberty. We propose to purchase a suitable permanent headquarters and enlist a competent staff to operate in the areas of research, publications, legal counseling and public relations. Our organization must be carried to every state in the nation where local and state chapters under qualified leadership can meet the issues with candor and dispatch.

I was present on this occasion and recall how Archer's promise of an expanding organization and activity electrified his audience. Yet it all seemed somewhat unrealistic and far away. The financial goal, in particular, seemed fantastic. It need not have seemed so. It did not seem so to Archer. As always, he set out to make his dream a fact. Every one of the goals he projected has been realized. The financial goal which seemed so far out of reach has been achieved many times over.

Three of the original chapters eventually developed into full-fledged regional offices with their own professional staffs. The regional offices are closely integrated with national, however, and the movement remains strongly centralized. The regional offices are in New York, Chicago and Los Angeles. Then come the chapters themselves with their officers, boards of directors and local programs. Next are committees which have not attained to chapter stature but are on the way. We have found from long experience that if we have any kind of local in a community, however feeble it may be, we are in an infinitely stronger position when some local problem erupts.

Another development in organization has been the semi-office or "clearing house" as it is sometimes called. The clearing house usually has a part-time official in charge, often a retired clergyman or lawyer. It serves as an agency for the national organization, solicits memberships, provides consultation in local church-state problems, channels information and keeps in close touch with the national office. As this was written clearing houses were in operation in Philadelphia, Boston, St. Louis and Baton Rouge. These have been subject to change, however, being set up and discontinued as local situations seemed to warrant. There are also field men. They may be full-time personnel attached to the national office, or they may be local leaders who are able to accept special assignments in places of special need for a limited period.

Then finally, some communities have study clubs that meet regularly for the study of church-state literature and problems. It is the locals which keep us informed about church-state situations that need reporting or action. I am always amused when one of the "clipping services" solicits our business. These are groups which specialize in clipping relevant items of interest from the nation's press and supplying them to the subscriber. I am amused and grateful, too, for we have a far more effective and comprehensive service of the kind and it costs us absolutely nothing. In virtually every major center of the country, and in hundreds of minor centers as well, are the friends of Americans United who faithfully provide a clipping and information service for which no group could afford to pay. When somebody gets out of line on church and state the chances are we shall know of it very promptly. Indeed, our problem is not a dearth of information but rather that of finding the time and the staff to keep up with our multiplicity of sources.

We have, also, in many areas persons who will ferret out specialized information for us in regard to local problems. This saves Americans United the expense of countless field trips of an investigatory nature. Our members supply us with the preliminary raw material which guides our decision as to whether a full-fledged, on-the-spot investigation by a staff member is warranted. This not only saves expense but actually enhances our effectiveness many times. It is this feature of organization which bestows upon Americans United its image of ubiquity. Wherever there is a church-state controversy, the chances are we know about it and are seeking to resolve it or, if it comes to battle, to winning it.

It has been noted that the founders and subsequent board members could not give a great deal of time and leadership to their movement. This is true but not the whole truth. The full board met only twice a year, but it created an executive committee whose members resided in the Washington area that could meet on call of the executive director. One of the most faithful and useful members of this committee was Rear Admiral Harold C. Fitz (USN Ret) who also served as treasurer of the corporation. Admiral Fitz, a war hero, is a Christian Scientist who served as a reader in his church. He has been a steady and faithful hand. The contribution he has made to Americans United over a 15-year period has been enormous. Dr. W. Kenneth Haddock, who long served as secretary, Dr. Theodore Henry Palmquist, a Methodist minister, Dr. Clyde W. Taylor, executive secretary of the National Association of Evangelicals, Dr. Frank W. Blackwelder, an Episcopal rector, and Dr. W. Melvin Adams and Dr. John C. Thompson, Adventist leaders, were helpful members of this small executive group. Leaders who were highly influential on the governing board at an early period were Elmer Rogers, Dr. Frank H. Yost, Dr. Charl Ormond Williams, Dr. Edward B. Willingham.

The long time chairman of the executive committee has been Dr. Walter Pope Binns who retired after 20 years in the presidency of William Jewell College in Missouri, and came to Washington, D. C. to live. His retirement was brief, for Americans United sat on his doorstep and implored him to come on the board. This he did. Next to having the wise leadership of our own president, Dr. Louie D. Newton, constantly available, that of Walter Pope Binns is the best. He is astute, incisive— and any other words one might use to indicate getting to the point and getting things done smoothly and quickly. He is a very wise man.

Dr. Newton a former president of the Southern Baptist Convention and pastor of Druid Hills Church in Atlanta, succeeded Charles Clayton Morrison as president and continues in this post. Perhaps his ablest associates on the board are also prominant Baptists. They are Dr. Dick Houston Hall, vice president of Atlanta Baptist College, Atlanta, Ga., and Dr. E. S. James, editor of the *Baptist Standard* of Texas. Not behind them are Dr. W. Melvin Adams of the Seventh-day Adventist Department of Religious Liberty and Dr. W. Stanley Rycroft, an executive with the Board of Ecumenical Missions of the United Presbyterian Church, USA. Dr. Clyde W. Taylor, a founder, continues his share of the direction of Americans United as a valued member both of its trustees and its executive committee.

These men whom we have always felt free to call as we had need, together with our executive committee whose members were frequently summoned when critical policy decisions had to be made, constituted the effective leadership of Americans United and the center of its effort. So long as he was in Washington, Dr. Joseph Martin Dawson, executive director of the Baptist Joint Committee on Public Affairs, was one of our indefatigables. I once wrote about Dr. Dawson that he had the happy faculty of being right on more things than any man I knew. That still goes, for Dr. Dawson, hale in his eighties, still travels to board meetings.

Dr. Charles Clayton Morrison, another of our emeritus board members, author of the *Manifesto,* died as these pages were in preparation. Dr. Morrison, for 37 years editor of the *Christian Century*, was perhaps the greatest single influence in the formation of Americans United. He was the intellectual force that shaped the *Manifesto* and, with J. M. Dawson and John A. Mackay, gave close attention to the organization's strategy in the early years. Dr. Morrison lived to 91 and remained clear and astute in his thinking. He frequently visited national headquarters and gave us the benefit of his counsel.

Most of the educational effort of Americans United has been devoted to the printed page and the lecture platform. Glenn Archer has averaged about 200 speeches a year during his tenure with Americans United. Other members of the staff have done almost as many. The pamphlet or folder bearing a message on church-state separation has become the trade mark of Americans United. The organization distributes them by the millions. It is safe to say that no group in the United States today carries on a comparable distribution of such items. *Church and State,* the organization's monthly journal, typically prints between 160,000 and 250,000. The circulation more than doubled during 1960 and has had a less rapid rise during the years since.

TV and radio provide a field that is gradually opening to staff members of Americans United. We have participated in numerous local interview and dialogue programs on church-state matters and have been on the networks as well. What commends us is the known fact that when someone is needed to defend the historic concept of strict separation of church and state Americans United can be counted on for a man who will provide an articulate and polished performance.

We are frequently asked, in view of the recent defeats for church-state separation on the national scene and in the states as well, whether our local organizations will not tend to level off and to decline. The exact opposite has already been indicated and for an obvious reason. Legislation such as the Economic Opportunity Act of 1964, the Elementary and Secondary Education Act of 1965, the National Defense Education Act of 1958 (often renewed) and the Higher Education Facilities Act of 1963, and others that could be mentioned, have tended to create church-state controversies in many communities. Last year we had more than 600 appeals from local communities for aid in correcting what appeared to local observers to be constitutional violations in the church-state area. Whereas there used to be a score of "trouble spots" that Glenn Archer kept in a couple of convenient files, today there are hundreds.

I should be astonished if this trend did not continue. I anticipate that it will continue at an ever escalating rate over the coming decade. This is why we are enlarging our staff and erecting a new headquarters building.

Where people call for our services there our organizational structure begins to take its rise. The more calls, the more organization. In formulation now is a program for a state director in every state of the Union and a rapid increase in the 150 chapters we now have to a thousand. The battle is by no means over. We have scarcely begun to fight.

Dr. Louie D. Newton, President of Americans United, and Dr. Walter Pope Binns, as the latter was honored by a Religious Liberty Citation in St. Louis, 1959.

chapter # XI NOW THE FUTURE

What is the future of Americans United for Separation of Church and State? Will it yet fall of its own weight as the Roman Catholic bishops predicted would happen by the end of its first year? Will the professional Protestant boardsmen be able to do-it-in as a few of them fondly hope? Will a clerical power be able one day to manipulate the state into suppressing it? Will it be able to stand the shock of a transfer of the reins of power from old hands to young hands as will be necessary within a few years?

These are all relevant questions and the future alone can provide the sure answers. But there is one question that encompasses and transcends all of these. That is the question: Has Americans United a necessary role to play in the United States today? The answer to that question is easy: It has. It is true that the outer defenses of church-state separation have been overrun by the enemy and that we shall be battling now in defense of the inner citadel.

Roman Catholic Action has gone a long way toward enforcing its demands for subsidy and special privilege upon the American public. Catholic denominational schools have now received recognition as an official part of the country's educational system. Children attending Catholic schools must receive federal assistance (as the aid to these institutions is presently being described) before any such assistance can be given to the public schools. This formula the Federal Government will now seek to impose upon state and local governments. Under "anti-poverty" and "defense" programs, public funds are being siphoned off to Protestant and Catholic institutions. There will be a hundred battles over this in the courts. Thousands of communities will be convulsed with inter-creedal antagonisms as professional brotherhooders rush about trying to get everyone to accept what they seem to regard as inevitable—subsidies to church institutions. There will be one legislative battle after another as sectarians, having pried the door ajar, will seek to force it wide open. One state after another will become a battleground as sectarians will boldly attack the constitutional provisions which have guaranteed separation of church and state at the money line.

All this is assuredly coming. It is already upon us. None but the most irresponsible foes of church-state separation would deny the significance of our role in the erupting controversy. We are practically alone as official defenders of the church-state tradition that has prevailed for the past century and a half in the United States. Palms of church boardsmen are itching for government money for their institutions. Clerical sociologists are eager for what they call a "partnership with the state" in the work of welfare and education. They want the state to tax the population to enhance their institutions and them. For are they not performing worthwhile works which involve a public purpose? What could God do if He had the money!

The Catholic hierarchy, flushed with its triumphs of the early nineteen sixties, will not rest. As has always been true, these triumphs will prove an incentive for more. The "consensus" which we now see among welfare staters, the Catholic leadership and Protestant institutionalists, will persist and grow more formidable until it breaks up in a squabble over the spoils.

Some of the Protestant leadership, particularly to the center and right of the theological spectrum, will continue to believe in money line separation of church and state and to defend it. It is possible that growing numbers of Catholic laymen, and even some clergy, disgusted with the predatory tactics of their own leadership, may begin to oppose the ambitious hierarchy. But among the rising elements of opposition there will be no single, clear voice consistently defending the tight, money line concept of separation, except that of Americans United.

The fact that some outer defenses have fallen is no reason to demobilize the army. The army is needed more than ever and it should be supplied and equipped adequately for the bruising encounter ahead. Even those who want to breach the wall of separation part way do not want to see it totally demolished.

They will presently be ranging themselves along side us. There is no where else for them to go.

The unchurched will be a substantial factor in the ultimate resolution of this struggle. There are some 65 million of them in the United States. They have never bothered to join a church; they will not relish a tax for religious institutions. Sparked by these people and joined by millions within the churches as well, there may well develop a new attitude toward the church as an institution.

One of the significant factors in this development will be the burgeoning of religious tax-exempt land and business. This is now accelerating at such a pace that it gives signs of getting completely out of hand. The study *Tax-Exempt Religious Property in Key American Cities*, prepared for Americans United by Dr. Martin A. Larson in 1964, showed this trend very clearly. The study showed that a number of our principal cities are nearing the point where half their land is tax-exempt. To be sure, government is a greater culprit than the churches but churches account for an amount of tax exemption that is rapidly on the rise, both absolutely and relatively.

The spectacle of oppressive increases in his taxes while church property and church commercial operations are not taxed at all is not designed to stir the non-churchman's admiration for the church. Nor, for that matter, is it pleasing to the layman himself. Add to this the prospect of billions of tax dollars flowing into church enterprises and you have the sure basis for anticlericalism. All of this gives the church a "bad image."

Today church popularity is on the wane. Occasionally this becomes overt as in the violent attacks directed from almost every quarter against the National Council of Churches. For the most part, however, it is inchoate and subliminal. It can be sensed in sly digs at the church. Churches which were once sacrosanct, able to reside behind a protective armor of general public approbation, now begin to feel the sting of criticism. Every week, now, articles reach us raising questions about tax exemption for the churches. Suits are filed in the courts challenging the entire concept. Perhaps this is as it should be. Certainly it is only what could be expected. Individuals and institutions which enter the political arena can expect to face the consequences. Those who strive for political emoluments and obtain them must be prepared for the penalties which they entail. If the churches continue their present drive for cooperation with government patronage and preferment from the state, then they will presently become merely another of the competitive groups struggling within the political process for their "share" or a little more. They will then be treated as such.

As this kind of "anti-clerical" reaction proceeds, the role of Americans United will become more and more significant. There must be no Mexican experience here! There must be no French or Russian Revolution! The reaction in Mexico was so violent that to this day the government owns all church property, and clergymen are forbidden by law to appear on the streets clad in clerical garb. This must not happen here. Americans United is equipped to head the kind of sane, responsible movement for separation of church and state that is imperatively needed. Anti-church sentiment must not be permitted to become hostility to religion itself. Americans United is a paradox: It is the hard-hitting enemy of official favoritism for the churches, yet it is and will always remain friendly to the churches.

Americans United has done far more than oppose the institutional build-up of the churches at the expense of the taxpayer. It has also stood forthrightly for the independence of religion from the state. It has always insisted that every opportunity be given to the churches under the "free exercise" clause of the First Amendment. Its record here is clear and it will reassure clergymen and laymen who refuse to join the "consensus" seeking to scuttle separation of church and state.

Now in the making is a mighty movement. It is a resurgence of the sentiment which inspired and created the doctrine of separation of church and state. Those who read these pages must never suspect that this is a negative movement. It is a movement which has its foes and these foes must be resolutely opposed. It is a movement that will strike massively at the "consensus" which seeks to merge into an obscurant union the church and the state. It will resolutely denounce and oppose those who would turn the churches into a minor branch of the United States Department of Health, Education and Welfare. It will oppose such leaders whether they button their collars before or behind.

Yet, fundamentally this is a positive movement. It supports one of the most profound and useful political concepts ever developed among mankind. It is more than that. It is a positive and effective way of handling the most delicate of human relationships. It is a way of preserving in respect and esteem all those convictions which cluster deep in the hearts of men. This concept of separation of church and state has been too pervasive for too long to be given up in a decade. It will not be given up. Those who seek to revive the archaic union of state and church with the pretext that it is something brave and new will receive the repudiation they deserve. The religious establishment will be no more palatable in its welfare garb than in the garb of the inquisition. The reason: We now know something better. We have had it and enjoyed it for a century and a half. It must be preserved for generations yet unborn as the finest portion of our heritage.

As we contemplate the future we have every reason to be encouraged. Our movement has steadily grown through the years. Not so fast as we had hoped, but it has forged ahead. Financial support has been loyal and consistent. The staff has been steadily enlarged as support and demands grew. Now we have purchased a desirable site and have taken on the project of a new building to replace our long outgrown headquarters on Massachusetts Avenue in Washington. The new building will symbolize the institutional stability and permanence of Americans United. It will stand as a functional memorial to the nation's founding fathers as well as to a devoted group of men in the 1940's who saw the need for a permanent organization to defend separation of church and state and did something about it.

With two decades safely weathered, we face the third with confidence and determination.

Some of America's outstanding religious and educational leaders share this dream. In the forefront of the effort to build a greater Americans United are the members of the current Board of Trustees: W. Melvin Adams, Jimmy R. Allen, Harold G. Basden, Walter Pope Binns, Frank W. Blackwelder, Harold C. Fitz, Edwin R. Garrison, Dick Houston Hall, Jr., E. S. James, Louie D. Newton, W. Stanley Rycroft, Herbert S. Southgate, Clyde W. Taylor, John C. Thompson, and Foy Valentine.

C. Stanley Lowell, associate director Americans United, Mrs. Elin M. Winn, donor of the Winn Memorial Library to be located in the projected headquarters building of Americans United, and Glenn L. Archer, the organization's executive director.

Dr. Louie D. Newton, president of Americans United, with A. John Fulton, inspector general for Georgia, Scottish Rite Masons, Southern Jurisdiction.

Dr. Newton with Dr. Searcy Garrison, executive secretary of the Baptist Convention of Georgia, and the first "Scroll Church" donor to Americans United when he served as pastor of the Bull Street Baptist Church, Savannah, Georgia.

BIBLIOGRAPHY

Basic Documents Relating to the Religious Clauses of the First Amendment, Americans United, Washington, D. C. 1965

Blanshard, Paul, *American Freedom and Catholic Power* (1958 Edition) Beacon Press, Boston

Blanshard, Paul, *God and Man in Washington,* Beacon Press, Boston, 1960

Blanshard, Paul, *Religion and the Schools: The Great Controversy,* Beacon Press, Boston 1963

Booth, James T., *Church Educational Problems in the State of California,* Catholic Book Agency, Rome, 1960

Bouscaren, T. Lincoln, S.J. and Ellis, Adams C., S.J., *Canon Law, A Text and Commentary,* Bruce Publishing Co., Milwaukee, 1958

Blum, Virgil C., S.J., *Freedom of Choice in Education,* the Macmillan Co., New York City, 1958

Blum, Virgil C., S.J., *Freedom in Education: Federal Aid for All Children,* Doubleday, Garden City, 1965

Brant, Irving, *James Madison,* Bobbs-Merrill, New York City, 1950

Butts, R. Freeman, *The American Tradition in Religion and Education,* Beacon Press, Boston, 1950

Creedon, Lawrence P. and Falcon, Wm. D., *United for Separation,* Bruce Pub. Co., Milwaukee, 1959

Curry, James E., *Public Regulation of the Religious Use of Land,* Michie Co., Charlottesville, Va. 1964

Davis, John Denis, *The Moral Obligations of Catholic Civil Judges,* Catholic University Press, Washington, D. C., 1953

Dawson, Joseph Martin, *Separate Church and State Now,* Richard R. Smith, New York City, 1948

Dawson, Joseph Martin, *A Thousand Months to Remember,* Baylor University Press, Waco, Texas 1964

Dilliard, Irving, *One Man's Stand for Freedom: Mr. Justice Black and the Bill of Rights,* Alfred A. Knopf, New York City, 1965

Douglas, William O., *The Bible and the Schools,* Little-Brown, New York City, 1966

Drinan, Robert F., S.J., *Religion, the Courts and Public Policy,* McGraw-Hill Book Co., New York, 1963

Healy, Edwin F., *Medical Ethics,* Loyola University Press, Chicago, 1956

Johnson, Alvin W. and Yost, Frank H., *Separation of Church and State in the United States,* U. of Minnesota Press, Minneapolis, 1948

Kauper, Paul G., *Religion and the Constitution*, Louisiana State University Press, 1964

Konvitz, Milton R., *Fundamental Liberties of a Free People*, Cornell University Press, 1957

La Noue, George A., *Public Funds for Parochial Schools?*, Dept. of Religious Liberty, National Council of Churches, New York City, 1963

Larson, Martin A., *Church Wealth and Business Income*, Philosophical Library, New York, 1965

Guenter, Lewy, *The Catholic Church and Nazi Germany*, McGraw-Hill Book Co., New York, 1964

Lowell, C. Stanley, *Federal Aid to Parochial Schools* (Congressional Testimony) Americans United, Washington, D.C., 1961

Lowell, C. Stanley, *Federal Aid to Parochial Schools: Questions of Constitutionality and Social Desirability*, Phi Delta Kappan, May, 1962

Lowell, C. Stanley, *Protestant-Catholic Marriage*, Broadman Press, Nashville, 1962

Lowell, C. Stanley, and Southgate, Herbert S., *Position Paper on Church-State Relations*, Americans United, Washington, D.C., 1961

Mackay, John A., *Ecumenics, The Science of the Church Universal*, Prentice-Hall, 1964

Manhattan, Avro, *Vatican Imperialism in the Twentieth Century*, Lyle Stuart, New York, 1965

McLoughlin, Emmett, *American Culture and Catholic Schools*, Lyle Stuart, New York, 1960

Moehlman, Conrad H., *The Wall of Separation*, Beacon Press, Boston, 1951

National Catholic Almanac, 1965, Doubleday & Co., New York

O'Donnell, Thomas J., *Morals in Medicine*, Newman Press, 1959

Official Catholic Directory, 1965, P. J. Kenedy & Sons, New York

Pfeffer, Leo, *This Honorable Court*, Beacon Press, Boston, 1965

Pfeffer, Leo, *Church State and Freedom*, Beacon Press, Boston, 1953

Ryan, Mary Perkins, *Are Parochial Schools the Answer? Catholic Education in the Light of the Council*, Holt, Rinehart & Winston, New York, 1963

Salisbury, Franklin C., *The Separationist Position on Church-State Relations*, Americans United, Washington, D.C., 1965

Stokes, Anson Phelps, *Church and State in the United States* (3 Volumes), Harper & Bros., New York, 1950

BIBLIOGRAPHY

Stokes, Anson Phelps, and Pfeffer, Leo, *Church and State in the United States*, Harper & Row, New York, 1964

Stuber, Stanley I., *Primer on Roman Catholicism for Protestants*, N. Y. Association Press, New York, 1965

Studies in Church-State Relations, Americans United, Washington, D.C., 1964

Thayer, V. T., *Religion in Public Education*, Viking Press, New York, 1947

Tussman, Joseph, *The Supreme Court on Church and State*, Oxford Press, New York, 1962

Yearbook of American Churches for 1965, edited by Benson Y. Landis, National Council of Churches, New York

INDEX (Quoted matter is marked q.)